THE WRITING PROGRAM 7

DAVID BOOTH / BOB CAMERON / PAT LASHMAR

THE WRITING PROGRAM 7

Modern Curriculum Press
Cleveland Toronto

ISBN 0-8136-1858-4

Editor: Elma Schemenauer
Designer: John Zehethofer

0 9 8 7 6 5 93

To the Student

If you had enough money to design and build any type of unusual "hobby home" you wished, what would it be? A fancy tree house? A grass hut? A houseboat? A longhouse? A house on stilts? A house in a cave? The choice you make probably reflects important aspects of your personality.

Designing and building your home would allow you to be creative, and would give you a chance to exercise many different skills. The final result would depend largely on how creative and hard-working you were.

In many ways, writing is like building a home. What you choose to write usually depends on your personality. The quality of the result usually depends on how imaginative and industrious you are.

However, just as in building a home you would probably seek some assistance, it is often wise to seek help in writing. Few beginners automatically know how to write well — just as few beginners would know how to build a house all by themselves. Some rare people, perhaps, are lucky. They seem to acquire writing skills with very little effort. Most of us, however, become proficient in writing mostly through step-by-step learning, reinforced by step-by-step practice.

The Writing Program is organized to help you develop writing concepts and skills, step by step. Each chapter begins with an introduction and a model selection or group of short selections. The models prepare you for the discussions and activities found within the chapters.

Each chapter gives easy-to-understand suggestions on planning, revising, editing, and sharing your writing. Also, each chapter provides you with ample opportunities to improve your other language arts skills: reading, listening, speaking, drama, representing, and viewing. Writing is important, but it should not be studied as an isolated subject. *The Writing Program* helps you develop your writing abilities — while at the same time enlarging your awareness, appreciation, and use of language in all its aspects.

Few published authors think about the nuts and bolts, or basics, of writing while writing their first drafts. All they think of is getting their ideas down. Most of the basics are already "in their bones," so they do not need to concentrate on them.

If professional writers make errors in the basics of writing, they usually correct these as they revise and polish their work. How do the professionals get the basics "into their bones?" Throughout this book are exercises and assignments designed to help you develop the professional's "feel" for writing.

The Writing Program presents many approaches to writing. Not all writers proceed in the same way. By trying different methods, you discover which are best for you.

Here are some suggestions you may find productive as you use this book:

1. Keep a writing folder of all written assignments. Every now and then, review your work and see which of your writing skills have improved and which still need work. In your writing folder, you can also keep "high interest" materials that you discover in your day-to-day reading. Use these sources to enrich, challenge, and inspire your own writing.
2. Keep a journal, noting interesting ideas and observations for writing. Refer to it frequently, especially when you need help in getting started on a piece of writing.
3. Learn how to utilize the many resources for writing. These include dictionaries, a thesaurus, encyclopedias, reference books, travel folders, magazines, and examples of outstanding writing done by others.
4. Revise, edit, proofread, and polish your work. Remember, even the professionals do it — sometimes many times over. Each chapter gives specific suggestions for improving pieces of writing done in that chapter. Also, at the back of this book, you will find helpful general checklists for revision.
5. Strive for a feeling of continual growth and progress in your writing.
6. As often as possible, share, publish, and display your work. After all, writing *is* communicating!

Contents

Transcriptions

Start the Tape Recorder

A transcription is a written record of oral talk; for example, a conversation, a court trial, or an improvised dialogue. Writing down speech gives you practice in listening carefully — as well as in spelling, punctuation, and capitalization. You can use transcriptions as a basis for developing your own compositions — editing, arranging, and structuring the ideas to suit yourself.

To Be Rich . . . or Poor

Do you think that life would be more fun if you were rich or if you were poor?

Jan, 12: Each one has its advantages and its disadvantages. Just because you are rich doesn't mean you are happy. When you are rich, I think it's harder. Rich people are pretty messed up, at least the ones I know are, and they are not very happy with the life they lead.

I think rich people wouldn't have anyone to talk to. The friends I have are very nervous about talking. They have to hide their weaknesses because they figure, "I have a lot of money, so there shouldn't be anything wrong with me. I'm rich, I'm not supposed to have any problems." Poor people *know* they've got problems, so they talk to their friends about it.

Louis, 11: Jan may have a point there, but I'd much prefer to be rich. If you were a rich person and you come upon a poor person and you both walk to the same store and want to buy the same things, the poor person is going to wonder, "Do I have enough money to get this thing?" They want to get this thing for a certain person they love. The rich person could get that thing for the person. Besides, rich people have a better chance of getting their goals in life — going on to a good college that could teach you a good trade. . . .

Jan, 12: I think money is a great thing to have, it helps a lot. But to be *born* rich, you'll be used to getting your way and that isn't how life is. I think it's much better if you are born poor, go to college, get a good job, and *then* become wealthy. It will change you some, but you are not going to become some stuck-up snob. If you just think about material value, you are really out of it!

Larry, 11: The rich *do* have more advantages, but you know poor people have their own advantages too. Poor people, if they have a friend, then you know it's a true friend — not when they're bored they just want to use your money. They'll be your friend because they *want* to be your friend.

Mike, 10: Some of my favorite games you don't need anything to play except some friends. So it may be fun to be poor because you don't do anything except play with your friends really. But if you are rich, you go out and buy something and you come home by yourself.

Jan, 12: If you are poor, it is much easier to mix with people, because you don't have much money and your friends don't have money and they don't care about that, you just get along. Also being rich, it's hard to tell if your friends like you for who you are, or for what you've got.

Felipe, 12: A rich person mixes in with a bunch of middle-class kids and they think, "He acts all uppity and he thinks he's too good for us, let's leave him alone." A poor kid would mix in with everything and everybody. He'd know how to get along with people in the middle class and lower class. A rich person would start bringing up all that his family did in the past, and he'd get people bored. Plus he couldn't tell if people liked him or not.

Supposing they go out after school, everybody's expecting him to buy them something, and if he doesn't, he's going to be the talk of the school. "You know so and so, he's so rich and he didn't even buy us anything at the pizza parlor." He won't have any friends left. If they thought he had a lot of money, they would really try to take advantage of him — try to get all the money they could out of him.

Mike, 10: Poor people probably have more friends, 'cause there are more poor people than there are rich people.

BUILDING A WRITING CONTEXT

1. **What viewpoints do the speakers in these transcriptions represent?**
2. **With whom did you agree most? Why?**
3. **Did reading the transcription change your own ideas?**
4. **When might you wish you had a transcript of what you and other people said?**

THE WRITING WORKSHOP

Preparing to Write

Usually transcripts are records of real conversations — or parts of real conversations. However, they may also be wholly or partially fictional.

Developing the Writing

1. Working in a small group, brainstorm a list of issues that you and your friends could discuss. As a group choose one topic that you would like to talk about and record.
2. Once your group has chosen a topic to discuss, use a tape or cassette recorder to record the conversation. You may continue the conversation for as long as you like, even though you may later choose to transcribe only a portion of it.
3. After you have completed the conversation, you are ready to transcribe it:
   - Play back and listen to the whole conversation.
   - Decide which parts of the talk you would like to write out. Each person speaking on the recording could be transcribed by one member of your group.
   - You will have to start and stop the tape several times in order to get the exact wording down.

- Take care to note who said what in the conversation, so that in fact your writing looks like a script.

Revising and Editing

Transcribing conversation demands careful attention to the conventions of print — spelling, capitalization, punctuation, and handwriting.

Exchange papers with a classmate. Copyedit each other's papers, marking any errors. Talk about how to correct them, and then do it.

Sharing and Publishing

Have another group read aloud the transcriptions that your group wrote. As you listen, note the effectiveness of your transcriptions. How could they be made even more effective? Make any improvements that seem appropriate.

Growing from Writing

A. Tape-record a conversation during lunch with your friends, or during dinner with your family. Prepare the participants to let them know that the conversation will be recorded. Later, transcribe the most interesting parts of the conversation into written form.

B. For this conversation, work in a group of about eight students. One of you is a magazine reporter who is doing a feature article on famous people. The reporter has been given an opportunity to interview a famous person for only five minutes in order to gather information for the article.

Another group member decides which famous person he or she would like to role-play. This person can be alive or dead, real or fictitious.

As the two group members carry out the five-minute interview, the others tape-record it and/or take notes.

Later, half the group transcribes parts of the conversation to be included with the feature article. The other half writes the article itself. In order to write the article, it may be necessary to do some further research on the famous person being featured.

Cartoons and Comic Strips

I Was Framed

Comic strips and cartoons give you a chance to write dialogue, both to amuse people and to make important points. Comic strips are usually made up of several boxes, or frames — while a cartoon may be a single frame. Often dialogue is contained in "speech balloons." However, as you can see from the following example, there are no hard and fast rules for the formats of cartoons and comic strips.

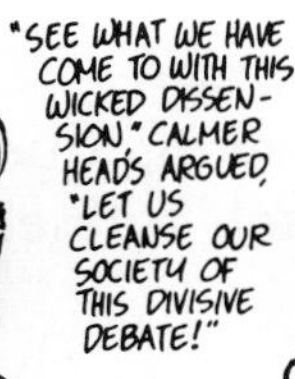

BUILDING A WRITING CONTEXT

1. What do you think the cartoonist is making fun of?
2. In this cartoon, which are more important — the pictures or the words?
3. How is the format of this selection different from the formats of other cartoons and comic strips that you have seen?

THE WRITING WORKSHOP

Preparing to Write

A cartoonist learns to say a great deal using only a few simple pictures and captions or dialogue. For your own cartoons, you can use sources of ideas such as jokes, riddles, issues that concern you, personal experiences, personal observations.

Developing the Writing

1. Decide which type of cartoon you wish to write:
   - Dialogue in balloons with no narration.
   - Monologue — words spoken by a single character.
   - Narrative caption or captions explaining what is happening.
2. Next select the material for your cartoon. Decide how many frames you will require. Begin by placing the words on your page.
3. Now design the artwork. Cartoons can be drawn in any style — from thumbprint characters to elaborate portraits. Pick a style that you can handle easily so that you can express your ideas without too much concern for drawing skills. You could even use pictures cut from newspapers and magazines.

Revising and Editing

Examine your cartoon for effect. Use the following questions.
1. Are there too few or too many words in each frame?
2. Do the drawings add to the impact?
3. Can you add or remove any words or pictures to give your strip more impact?

Sharing and Publishing

Share your comic strips as a class, perhaps by displaying them on a bulletin board or wall. What topics appear to be most popular?

Growing from Writing

A. Take a modern poem and recreate it as a comic strip.

B. Choose an unfortunate incident in your own life and recreate it as a comic strip.

C. As a class, select a topic. Each student designs a comic strip on this same topic. The collection can be displayed on a bulletin board, and the different approaches compared.

Radio Plays

Seeing with Your Ears

When radio first became popular in the 1920s, it brought information and entertainment to millions of listeners around the world. Using only various sounds as their tools — voices, music, sound effects, and silence — writers of radio programs created excitement and emotion over the airwaves.

The following is an example of a radio comedy script of the past. A Laurel and Hardy script, it involves:

- **Edgar, a justice of the peace (also called the Judge).**
- **Stan and Patsy, a couple planning to be married.**
- **Ollie, the couple's friend.**

As the excerpt begins, Edgar is performing the wedding ceremony.

The Wedding Party

EDGAR: . . . . Do you take this woman to be your lawfully wedded wife?
STAN: I — ah, don't think so.
EDGAR: Why not?
STAN: I've taken a dislike to her.
OLLIE: *(Incredulous.)* You've taken a *dislike* to her?
STAN: Yep. (SOUND: PATSY *crying, then fainting.*)
OLLIE: Quick, Judge. She's fainted.
STAN: Get her some brandy.
EDGAR: I haven't got any brandy.
PATSY: *(Quickly.)* A beer'll do.

STAN: You're a fine judge. No brandy! Huh!
EDGAR: Now, just a minute, just a minute. Did you or did you not wake me up out of a sound sleep to marry you?
STAN: I don't remember. (*Hiccups.*)
EDGAR: And now you stand there and say you don't want to go through with it?
STAN: Well, I'm sorry. I changed my mind. I couldn't help it.
EDGAR: (*Yells.*) Why, you little —
OLLIE: Come on, Patsy. Let's get out of here.
(SOUND: *party leaving for outside.*)
PATSY: (*Crying.*) Oh, Stanley, you brute.
STAN: I can't help it, Patsy. I just —
OLLIE: Stanley.
STAN: What, Ollie?
OLLIE: You came out here to get married, didn't you?
STAN: Yes.
OLLIE: You took poor little Patsy away from her mother — her home.
STAN: Yes, I know but —
OLLIE: You stood her up at the altar. Only a cad would do that.
STAN: (*Cries.*) I'm sorry. I —
OLLIE: Now we're going back in there and you're going to behave yourself.
STAN: Ollie.
OLLIE: What?
STAN: Give me another shot.
OLLIE: *(Disgustedly.)* Oh, here.
(SOUND: *gurgling gullet.*)
STAN: Oh, that's good, thank you.
OLLIE: Now kiss and make up.
(SOUND: *large suction effect.*)
Oh, not *me! Patsy!*
(SOUND: *bell.*)
EDGAR: Oh, so it's you again, eh?
OLLIE: Now everything's straightened out, Judge. I've talked to Stanley.
EDGAR: It better be. Come in. Now stand before me. Young man, do you take this woman to be your lawful wedded wife?
STAN: I do.
EDGAR: Fine. Now, young woman, do you take this man to be your lawful wedded husband?

PATSY: I should say not. I've taken a dislike to him.
STAN: Well, can you beat that?
EDGAR: Why, you two little whippersnappers, I'll take the both of you and wring your necks.
OLLIE: Come on, come on. Let's get out of here.
(SOUND: *party leaving for outside.*)
This is another fine mess you've gotten me into. Now look Patsy, you came out here to get married, didn't you?
PATSY: Sure.
OLLIE: You took poor little Stanley away from me. You broke up *my* home. You brought him all the way here to Las Vegas.
PATSY: (*Tearfully.*) Yes, I know.
OLLIE: And when you get here, you leave him standing at the altar. You ought to be ashamed of yourself.
PATSY: Oh, I'm sorry.
OLLIE: Now, kiss and make up.
(SOUND: *large suction effect.*)
Not *me! Stanley!* Now come on, let's go in.
STAN: Ollie.
OLLIE: What is it *now*?
STAN: What about another shot?
OLLIE: Not now.
PATSY: Make it two.
OLLIE: Wait until after you're married.
(SOUND: *bell.*)
STAN: (*To* JUDGE.) Surprise!
EDGAR: Surprise? Why, you —
OLLIE: Oh, calm down, Judge. Now everything is all settled.
EDGAR: Oh, it is, eh? Step right in, folks.
PATSY: Thank you, Judge.
EDGAR: Now stand before me. Do you take this man to be your lawful wedded husband?
PATSY: I do.
EDGAR: And do you take this woman to be your lawful wedded wife?
STAN: I do.
EDGAR: Well, I won't marry you!
OLLIE: Why not?
EDGAR: Because I've taken a dislike to the whole *bunch* of you!
OLLIE: But, Judge —
EDGAR: Get out of here!

(SOUND: *party leaving.*)
PATSY: Well, it looks like back to the laundry for me.
STAN: Ollie, what about that shot you promised me?
OLLIE: (*Sweetly.*) Oh, thank you, Stanley. I'm glad you reminded me. *Here* it is!!
(SOUND: *gunshot. Into theme, "The Dance of the Cuckoos."*)

BUILDING A WRITING CONTEXT

1. **If you were taking part in a performance of this script, which role would you like to play? Why?**
2. **What other sounds could be included as well as those indicated in the brackets?**
3. **Why do you think silence is considered a "sound" in radio broadcasting?**

THE WRITING WORKSHOP

Preparing to Write

Writing a radio play gives you an opportunity to create images in the listener's mind. Every sound and word you use will help build an imaginary world for the audience to explore. Often this kind of work is called "Theatre of the Mind."

You may decide to work with a partner or a small group to develop your radio play.

Developing the Writing

When words are heard over the radio, the audience has only sound to make meaning. It is the use of sound that can create excitement, dramatic emotion, humor, or whatever other response the writer seeks. The various sounds that the listeners hear are the tools of the radio script writer. These sounds can be voices, music, sound effects, and silence.

Read the following novel excerpt, thinking about how you could adapt it into a radio script.

from **Nobody's Family is Going to Change** Louise Fitzhugh

Emma trudged home heavily, her books seeming to weigh more than the day before. She was having a running argument with herself about the consumption of a cream horn, an additional, unnecessary cream horn, at lunch that day. The argument went through her head like this:

THE STATE OF NEW YORK
AGAINST EMANCIPATION SHERIDAN

DISTRICT ATTORNEY: Your name is Emancipation Sheridan, otherwise known to your friends and family as Emma Sheridan?

EMMA: Yes.

D.A.: Yes, Sir.

EMMA: Yes, Sir.

D.A.: Now, Emma, tell the jury what you had for lunch today.

EMMA: Hot dogs and sauerkraut.

D.A. *(snidely)*: And what else, Emma?

EMMA: Chocolate milk.

D.A. *(insinuating):* And?

EMMA *(looking down and whispering):* A roll.

D.A.: Now, Emma, you're evading the question. You realize that you're under oath. Are you going to swear under oath to the honest, upstanding ladies and gentlemen of the jury that that's *all* you had for lunch?

EMMA *(whispering even lower):* A cream horn.

D.A.: What? Speak up. We can't hear you.

EMMA (a bit louder): A cream horn.

D.A. (greatly irritated): Your honor, will you please direct this witness to answer my questions loudly and clearly so that the court and the jury can understand her?

JUDGE: Miss Sheridan, will you please try to speak up?

EMMA: Yes, sir.

JUDGE: What?

EMMA: Yes, sir.

D.A. *(swaggering around):* Now, Miss Sheridan, will you please tell the jury what else you ate for lunch.

EMMA: A cream horn.

D.A. (slyly): Do you want to leave it at that?

EMMA (yelling): Oh, all right, *two* cream horns.

Emma almost walked into a parking meter. She stopped herself just in time and trudged along, back in the real world now. Oh, the shame of it. Two cream horns.

Still, when she finally passed her bar exam and she finally had a case and she was cross-examining the school dietitian, it would go like this:

EMMA *(prominent young New York trial lawyer):* Did you or did you not put out a tray of forty cream horns — and don't say there weren't forty, because there were, because I counted them — did you or did you not put that tray out there to tempt and lead astray and in particular to ravage the diet of one Emma Sheridan?

DIETITIAN *(meekly):* I did.

EMMA: If it please the court, this witness refuses to speak up and I have failed in all my efforts to get her to speak louder.

JUDGE: We will have no more of that. Dietitian of the Gregory School, you *will* speak up.

Emma gave a smile of satisfaction. She watched the dietitian cringe and wiggle around for a minute, then own up to her own crime. Her mother's voice broke through her dream: Just because there were forty, that didn't mean that you had to eat forty, Emma. It didn't mean that you even had to eat *one*.

The shame of it. It was nobody's fault but her own that she ate like a horse and looked like a pig, so much so that everybody called her Piggy. At first she hadn't minded. There was a friendly sound to the name. As she got fatter and fatter, however, she realized that there wasn't anything friendly about it. It was merely a descriptive term for that most shameful of all things, a FATGIRL.

Using the excerpt from *Nobody's Family is Going to Change*, work with a partner or small group to prepare a five-minute radio script, following the same format as the Laurel and Hardy script. You do not have to use the whole novel excerpt. Consider these questions:

1. Which parts would you want to eliminate? To change? To add to?
2. How many characters are needed?
3. How often do you wish the narrator or narrators to speak?
4. How will the narrators help the listeners understand what is happening?
5. Can the narrator be a character from the story?
6. How can you clearly convey to the listeners where this scene is taking place?
7. How can sound effects best be used?
8. How can music help the presentation before, during, or after the reading of the script?
9. What kind of directions will you give for the way you want the characters to say their lines? Examples: *quickly, incredulous, yelling, crying.*
10. Will you give directions for pauses, or silent moments?

Revising and Editing

In order to edit your work, it will be necessary to have your script read aloud. Ask a group of students to do this, following your directions. Those who are presenting the work will help you realize where you will have to clarify and extend points. Perhaps an extra small scene will be required to explain what is happening.

After you have heard your script read aloud, improve it in any ways that seem appropriate.

Sharing and Publishing

Again exchange your script with another group for sharing. Taping the plays will give you a chance to re-hear your work after the presentation. You can use the tape-recording as a demonstration of what you have created. You may also hear places where you would like to continue changing and adapting. Writing is a never-ending process.

Growing from Writing

A. Choose an excerpt from a novel that you are reading. With a partner or small group, prepare a radio script for a scene from this novel.

B. With a partner, create a radio script for a one-minute commercial selling a product that can be used in the home. Consider these questions:

1. How many characters will you need in your commercial?
2. Will you have a narrator or narrators?
3. How can you let the audience "see" the product without showing it to them?
4. What will the setting be for your commercial?
5. How will the listeners know who the characters are?

C. Prepare a radio script of a horror story or science fiction story, using many sound effects.

Humor

Saskatchewan Is All Right, Really

We need to be able to laugh at ourselves, to chuckle at our little faults and smile at our foolishness. People who can do this are better able to survive the storms and hardships of life.

Author Eric Nicol is one of Canada's most outstanding humorists. Nicol has a talent for making fun of people and events by greatly exaggerating the truth. In reading this story by Eric Nicol, note his use of exaggeration, his humorous tone, and his use of amusing language.

Land of the Gopher ERIC NICOL

Saskatchewan's capital city is Regina, which inconveniences gophers for an area of several square miles. Regina enjoys the distinction of being a self-made city, having erected all its own scenery, including a large artificial lake in which the residents can drown just as easily as if they lived on the coast.

Regina hasn't a tree she can call her own. Take away all the trees she's bought or had given to her, and she'd be nude as the day she was incorporated, and proud of it. For, it seems that there was nothing at Regina when the first pioneers rolled in with their covered wagons, except a couple of old cow skulls (too big for novelty ashtrays), and a lot of prematurely bald prairie. A person could see for miles in every direction, of course, but so could everybody else, so that you couldn't get away with a thing. . . .

Quickly organizing a Junior Board of Trade, the people of Regina recognized the fact that their town wasn't going to attract many tourists with a couple of old cow skulls and a mess of bald prairie where the tourists couldn't even work up a decent auto accident. So, they started importing trees, all kinds of trees, until they had thousands of them piled up on the platform of the railway station. At this point the question arose of who was to have the honor of planting the trees. Everybody proved very unselfish and self-effacing about this opportunity, some even going so far as to hide under their garage in order to forego the privilege.

The Junior Board of Trade wasted so much time nominating absent members to plant the trees that the dogs of Regina became thoroughly fed up with the whole affair. Many of these dogs had left fine trees in the East in order to come West and help keep alive the tradition that they were people's best friends (the horse was beginning to muscle in on the racket about that time), only to encounter procrastination in high places.

Finally the scheme was hit on inviting distinguished personages to Regina and having them plant trees to commemorate their visit. Some of these celebrities were called back again and again, barely getting home before they received another invitation: "The City of Regina begs the honor of your presence at the Warble Fly Festival next Friday. Please bring your shovel."

After a while these guests became a trifle suspicious of Regina's hospitality, and many thereafter gave the city a wide berth. . . . By then, however, enough trees had been planted to attract people from all over the prairies, people who had never seen a tree but thought they'd like to. From these, a Public Works Department was chosen to plant more trees, so that even today it is not uncommon to see a little group of people running around Regina with a sapling, looking for a place to plant it.

In fact, there has been some uneasy talk . . . of having to move a number of buildings out of town, in order to make room for the trees that continue to flood in from other parts of the country. One section of public opinion has developed that is definitely anti-tree, arguing that unless the mad influx of trees is halted, Regina will soon be lost in an impenetrable forest, never to be seen again.

BUILDING A WRITING CONTEXT

1. **A beginning, a middle, and an end — these are the parts of most good stories. The beginning of this story states the main characters' problem: their city had no trees. Using a sentence or two for each, summarize the middle and the end of the story.**
2. **What is the meaning of the title "Land of the Gopher?" If you need help, look up *gopher* in a dictionary or encyclopedia.**
3. **One example of exaggeration from the story is:**

   In fact, there has been some uneasy talk . . . of having to move a number of buildings out of town, in order to make room for the trees. . . .

   Find two other examples of exaggeration. Discuss why you would call them exaggeration.

THE WRITING WORKSHOP

Preparing to Write

Writing a humorous story is a lot like picking up that first handful of snow, patting it into shape, and creating a snowball. Then you begin to roll it around the yard and pick up more snow. It becomes a bigger ball and you begin to think about the snowman you are creating.

Where do you begin?

- Sometimes a character suggests a story. Or perhaps it's a group of characters, like the early citizens of Regina in "Land of the Gopher."
- Sometimes it's a place that sparks an idea.
- Sometimes it's something that happened to you in real life. The most successful writers are often those who can turn ordinary things in their lives into exciting adventures on paper.

It may be helpful to start planning by thinking of the overall story — beginning, middle, and end — which often have these functions:

- The beginning introduces the main characters and their problem.
- The middle tells what the main characters did and what happens.

- The end tells how the main characters solved their problem, and how the story ends.

Developing the Writing

A. Humorist Eric Nicol wrote the following description of Saskatchewan.

> Trapped in the middle of Canada crouches the Province of Saskatchewan. Saskatchewan is distinguished from other Provinces on the map by its good straight borders. All the other Provinces have a crooked side, as any Saskatchewanian will gladly, even heatedly, tell you. But, since it has no snow-capped mountains and is infested with small branch offices, Saskatchewan has always felt sensitive about its appearance. Thousands of ex-Saskatchewanians living in every other part of Canada stoutly defend the beauties of their home Province, without making any immediate plans to move back to it.
>
> Why? Well, for one thing, "Saskatchewan" is harder to spell. Oodles of people cannot spell "Saskatchewan." People resent living in a Province whose name they can't spell. Inquisitive persons are liable to ask them how to spell the name of their Province, and it is embarrassing for them not to know. After a while the more sensitive ones pack up and move to a more easily spelled place, like Ontario or British Columbia, and try to start life afresh.

Write your own humorous description of a town, city, or community.

B. Some writers say the only difference between humor and tragedy is the outcome. It is true that we tend to laugh and cry at the same things. If a situation ends well, it can be viewed from the distance of time as funny, regardless of mishaps along the way. In a paragraph, discuss an incident that bordered on both the comic and tragic. The incident may be from a book, a movie, or your own experience.

C. Based on the place you described in Activity A and/or the incident you discussed in Activity B, plan and write a humorous story. Make sure you have a beginning, middle, and end. Try to use exaggeration, a humorous tone, and amusing language — as Eric Nicol did in "Land of the Gopher."

D. The title of a story should tell what the story is about and make the reader want to read it. Just as a good joke doesn't give away the punch line before the ending, your title shouldn't give away any secrets in your story. Try out at least three titles for your story in Activity C. Finally, choose the best one.

Revising and Editing

After you have written your humorous story and before you start to edit, try putting it aside for a few days without looking at it. Let it "cool" so you will have a fresh perspective when you do edit it.

As you edit, ask yourself the following questions.

1. Does my story start at the most exciting beginning place?
2. Is there one complete story with a beginning, a middle, and an end?
3. Is the story logical — that is, does one thing follow another in a logical order?
4. Have I explained why things are happening? Everything necessary must be in the story — have I included all the explanations without giving so many details that the story becomes boring or confusing?
5. Is my ending strong? Does my story stop at the most dramatic point, or do I take too long explaining the ending? Have I solved the main character's or characters' problem?
6. Are my spelling and punctuation correct?

Sharing and Publishing

A number of writers have used humor to express viewpoints about history, geography, and politics. You may enjoy some of the following, which you should be able to find through a public library.

The Celebrated Jumping Frog of Calaveras County, by Mark Twain

How We Elect Our Presidents, by Will Rogers

Lake Wobegon Days, by Garrison Keillor

Son of the Great Society, by Art Buchwald

Fables

The Moral of the Story

Fables are usually short folktales about flaws in human kind, as seen from one point of view. Often they use animals to represent certain human types and end in a simple moral, or lesson.

What problems do the main characters have in the following fables? What lessons do they learn?

The Egg-eating Dog AESOP

There was a dog who was fond of eating eggs. Mistaking a shellfish for an egg one day, he opened his mouth wide and swallowed it down in one gulp. The weight of it in his stomach caused him intense pain. "Serves me right," he said, "for thinking that anything round must be an egg."

The Centipede's Errand

JAPANESE FABLE

Once a centipede, a flea, and a louse gathered together on a cold day.

"Why don't the three of us drink some wine together on a day like this?" the centipede suggested.

They all agreed, but then they had to decide which one would go to buy it.

The flea said, "I always jump along, *pinpin*, and the jug might get broken. I can't go on such an errand."

The louse said, "I walk *guzu-guzu*, terribly slow, so I am afraid I cannot be of any help."

There was nothing for the centipede to do but go himself.

No matter how long the flea and louse waited, the centipede did not come back. They got impatient and decided to see what he was up to. They found him busy doing something in the corner of the yard.

"Hey, Mister Centipede, what are you doing?" they called. "It's getting late."

Without turning around, he replied, "I have a lot of feet and I am still fastening sandals onto them."

BUILDING A WRITING CONTEXT

1. **What other very old fables have you read (perhaps by Aesop)? How does "The Centipede's Errand" compare with these?**
2. **What point of view does the moral at the end of "The Egg-Eating Dog" represent?**

THE WRITING WORKSHOP

Preparing to Write

A. There are many ways to begin writing a fable. Brainstorm all the standard fable characters you can think of; for example, the boaster, the trickster, the fool. What do you hope might happen to each of these characters in a fable?

With a partner, choose two of the fable characters you have brainstormed. Decide what animals you will choose to represent them; for example, a fox for a trickster, a rabbit for a fearful character. Then role-play a dialogue between the two concerning a simple situation, such as saving food for a rainy day. Try to keep some animal characteristics in your oral fable.

B. The following are some proverbs that could act as morals for fables. You can use one as a beginning point for making up a group fable.

- A warm smoke is better than a cold fog.
- A single line may have two hooks.
- Empty vessels loom biggest.
- Faroff cows wear long horns.

Discuss in a small group the meanings of some of these proverbs. Then decide upon a character who could represent a person who did not recognize the truth of the proverb.

Choose one proverb and tell a round-robin fable. Each person contributes one event or detail to the story. The person who concludes the story repeats the proverb that is its lesson, or moral.

Developing the Writing

As a basis for creating a fable, choose a modern problem that young people are faced with in today's society. It could be a difficult family situation, a school problem, a peer difficulty, or a career choice. Decide on at least two characters to use in your fable, and represent them with animal figures. Now write the fable as quickly as possible, letting the ideas flow from your pen. The following questions may serve as useful guides as you write:

- Where are the characters?
- Why are they there?
- What do they look like?
- What words do they speak?
- What details will help create vivid pictures in the reader's mind?

You are writing your fable for a class book of modern fables.

Now rewrite the same fable, but this time use one different character. For example, if you had a wimpish rabbit in your last version, try a shy mouse in this one. Search for the animal type that will help make your point the most strongly.

End your fable with a moral. You might try reversing an old moral, or making a play on words so that your fable has extra punch. Then make up a title to signal the subject of your fable, such as *The Wolf Who Cried Boy.*

Revising and Editing

A. Read your fable to a partner or to a small group. Ask the listeners to suggest details that would improve your fable. Make any of the suggested changes that you agree with.

B. Too many short sentences can sometimes make a piece of writing seem "choppy." How could the following short sentences be put together to make one longer, smoother sentence?

- The dog mistook a shellfish for an egg one day.
- He opened his mouth wide.
- He swallowed it down in one gulp.

Look back at "The Egg-eating Dog" to see how the author combined these thoughts.

Now reread your fable. Are there places where it seems "choppy?" Can you put any of your sentences together to create longer, smoother ones?

Sharing and Publishing (A Whole-class Activity)

Create a class book called *Modern Fables: A Manual for Surviving in Today's World.*

Design a cover for your book. You could use magazine illustrations to show the types of characters you have included in your writing.

Growing from Writing

A. Choose a rock video that you enjoy — one that tells a story. Then write a fable based on the video. Will there be a moral? Will you use animal characters?

B. Find a traditional fable in a book of folklore. Rewrite the fable as a problem that has been sent to an advice column in the newspaper.

C. Take a letter from an advice column in the newspaper and rewrite it as a fable.

D. These proverbs have been based on familiar ones that you probably know. Try to write down the original proverb in each case.

- A rotating fragment of minerals collects no bryophytic plants.
- Exercise your visual faculties prior to executing a jump.
- Under no circumstances compute the number of your barnyard fowl previous to their incubation.
- An excess of individuals skilled in the preparation of edibles impairs the quality of thin soup.
- A feathered biped in the terminal part of the arm equals in value a pair of feathered bipeds in densely branched shrubbery.
- A recently purchased implement for brushing away floor dirt invariably displaces the dirt most efficiently.

- A timorous heart at no time succeeds in acquiring the beautiful damsel.
- Everything is legitimate in matters pertaining to ardent affections and armed conflict between nations.

E. **Keeping a Journal**
Write a short fable about one difficult incident in your life this week. What character will you use to represent yourself? Perhaps you could write the moral in the form of a question that you would like to have answered.

Science Fiction

2026, Here We Come

In most of Ray Bradbury's writing, the theme is the effect upon human beings of a world made increasingly inhuman by human's own technology. One of Bradbury's best-known works, *The Martian Chronicles*, is an episodic novel. That is, the various chapters (published over a period of four years) may stand alone as separate, complete stories.

Bradbury's own favorite chronicle is "August 2026: There Will Come Soft Rains." The story depicts life in the last house standing amid the radioactive rubble after a world war.

August 2026: There Will Come Soft Rains RAY BRADBURY

In the living room the voice-clock sang, *Tick-tock, seven o'clock, time to get up, time to get up, seven o'clock!* as if it were afraid that nobody would. The morning house lay empty. The clock ticked on, repeating and repeating its sounds into the emptiness. *Seven-nine, breakfast time, seven-nine!*

In the kitchen the breakfast stove gave a hissing sigh and ejected from its warm interior eight pieces of perfectly browned toast, eight eggs sunnyside up, sixteen slices of bacon, two coffees, and two cool glasses of milk.

"Today is August 4, 2026," said a second voice from the kitchen ceiling, "in the city of Allendale, California." It repeated the date three times for memory's sake. "Today is Mr. Featherstone's birthday. Today is the anniversary of Tilita's marriage. Insurance is payable, as are the water, gas, and light bills."

Somewhere in the walls, relays clicked, memory tapes glided under electric eyes.

Eight-one, tick-tock, eight-one o'clock, off to school, off to work, run, run, eight-one! But no doors slammed, no carpets took the soft tread of rubber heels. It was raining outside. The weather box on the front door sang quietly: "Rain, rain, go away; rubbers, raincoats for today. . . ." And the rain tapped on the empty house, echoing.

Outside, the garage chimed and lifted its door to reveal the waiting car. After a long wait the door swung down again.

At eight-thirty the eggs were shriveled and the toast was like stone. An aluminum wedge scraped them into the sink, where hot water whirled them down a metal throat which digested and flushed them away to the distant sea. The dirty dishes were dropped into a hot washer and emerged twinkling dry.

Nine-fifteen, sang the clock, *time to clean.*

Out of warrens in the wall, tiny robot mice darted. The rooms were acrawl with the small cleaning animals, all rubber and metal. They thudded against chairs, whirling their mustached runners, kneading the rug nap, sucking gently at hidden dust. Then, like mysterious invaders, they popped into their burrows. Their pink electric eyes faded. The house was clean.

Ten o'clock. The sun came out from behind the rain. The house stood alone in a city of rubble and ashes. This was the one house left standing. At night the ruined city gave off a radioactive glow which could be seen for miles.

Ten-fifteen. The garden sprinklers whirled up in golden founts, filling the soft morning air with scatterings of brightness. The water pelted windowpanes, running down the charred west side where the house had been burned evenly free of its white paint. The entire west face of the house was black, save for five places. Here the silhouette in paint of a man mowing a lawn. Here, as in a photograph, a woman bent to pick flowers. Still farther over, their images burned on wood in one titanic instant, a small boy, hands flung into the air; higher up, the image of a thrown ball, and opposite him a girl, hands raised to catch a ball which never came down.

The five spots of paint — the man, the woman, the children, the ball — remained. The rest was a thin charcoaled layer.

The gentle sprinkler rain filled the garden with falling light.

Until this day, how well the house had kept its peace. How carefully it had inquired, "Who goes there? What's the password?" and, getting no answer from lonely foxes and whining cats, it had shut up its windows and drawn shades in an old-maidenly preoccupation with self-protection which bordered on a mechanical paranoia.

It quivered at each sound, the house did. If a sparrow brushed a window, the shade snapped up. The bird, startled, flew off! No, not even a bird must touch the house!

The house was an altar with ten thousand attendants, big, small, servicing, attending, in choirs. But the gods had gone away, and the ritual of the religion continued senselessly, uselessly.

Twelve noon.

A dog whined, shivering, on the front porch.

The front door recognized the dog voice and opened. The dog, once huge and fleshy, but now gone to bone and covered with sores, moved in and through the house, tracking mud. Behind it whirred angry mice, angry at having to pick up mud, angry at inconvenience.

For not a leaf fragment blew under the door but what the wall panels flipped open and the copper scrap rats flashed swiftly out. The offending dust, hair, or paper, seized in miniature steel jaws, was raced back to the burrows. There, down tubes which fed into the cellar, it was dropped into the sighing vent of an incinerator which sat like evil Baal in a dark corner.

The dog ran upstairs, hysterically yelping to each door, at last realizing, as the house realized, that only silence was here.

It sniffed the air and scratched the kitchen door. Behind the door, the stove was making pancakes which filled the house with a rich baked odor and the scent of maple syrup.

The dog frothed at the mouth, lying at the door, sniffing, its eyes turned to fire. It ran wildly in circles, biting at its tail, spun in a frenzy, and died. It lay in the parlor for an hour.

Two o'clock, sang a voice.

Delicately sensing decay at last, the regiments of mice hummed out as softly as brown gray leaves in an electrical wind.

Two-fifteen.

The dog was gone.

In the cellar, the incinerator glowed suddenly and a whirl of sparks leaped up the chimney.

Two thirty-five.

Bridge tables sprouted from patio walls. Playing cards fluttered onto pads in a shower of pips. Martinis manifested on an oaken bench with egg-salad sandwiches. Music played.

But the tables were silent and the cards untouched.

At four o'clock the tables folded like great butterflies back through the paneled walls.

Four-thirty.

The nursery walls glowed.

Animals took shape: yellow giraffes, blue lions, pink antelopes, lilac panthers cavorting in crystal substance. The walls were glass. They looked out upon color and fantasy. Hidden films clocked through well-oiled sprockets, and the walls lived. The nursery floor was woven to resemble a crisp, cereal meadow. Over this ran aluminum roaches and iron crickets, and in the hot still air butterflies of delicate red tissue wavered among the sharp aroma of animal spoors! There was the sound like a great matted yellow hive of bees within a dark bellows, the lazy bumble of a purring lion. And there was the patter of okapi feet and the murmur of a fresh jungle rain, like other hoofs, falling upon the summer-starched grass. Now the walls dissolved into distances of parched weed, mile on mile, and warm endless sky. The animals drew away into thorn brakes and water holes.

It was the children's hour.

Five o'clock. The bath filled with clear hot water.

Six, seven, eight o'clock. The dinner dishes manipulated like magic tricks, and in the study a *click*. In the metal stand opposite the hearth where a fire now blazed up warmly, a cigar popped out, half an inch of soft gray ash on it, smoking, waiting.

Nine o'clock. The beds warmed their hidden circuits, for nights were cool here.

Nine-five. A voice spoke from the study ceiling:

"Mrs. McClellan, which poem would you like this evening?"

The house was silent.

The voice said at last, "Since you express no preference, I shall select a poem at random." Quiet music rose to back the voice. "Sara Teasdale. As I recall, your favourite. . . .

"There will come soft rains and the smell of the ground,
And swallows circling with their shimmering sound;

And frogs in the pools singing at night,
And wild plum trees in tremulous white;

Robins will wear their feathery fire,
Whistling their whims on a low fence-wire;

And not one will know of the war, not one
Will care at last when it is done.

Not one would mind, neither bird nor tree,
If mankind perished utterly;

And Spring herself, when she woke at dawn
Would scarcely know that we were gone."

The fire burned on the stone hearth and the cigar fell away into a mound of quiet ash on its tray. The empty chairs faced each other between the silent walls, and the music played.

At ten o'clock the house began to die.

The wind blew. A falling tree bough crashed through the kitchen window. Cleaning solvent, bottled, shattered over the stove. The room was ablaze in an instant!

"Fire!" screamed a voice. The house lights flashed, water pumps shot water from the ceilings. But the solvent spread on the linoleum, licking, eating, under the kitchen door, while the voices took it up in chorus: "Fire, fire, fire!"

The house tried to save itself. Doors sprang tightly shut, but the windows were broken by the heat and the wind blew and sucked upon the fire.

The house gave ground as the fire in ten billion angry sparks moved with flaming ease from room to room and then up the stairs. While scurrying water rats squeaked from the walls, pistoled their water, and ran for more. And the wall sprays let down showers of mechanical rain.

But too late. Somewhere, sighing, a pump shrugged to a stop. The quenching rain ceased. The reserve water supply which had filled baths and washed dishes for many quiet days was gone.

The fire crackled up the stairs. It fed upon Picassos and Matisses in the upper halls, like delicacies, baking off the oily flesh, tenderly crisping the canvases into black shavings.

Now the fire lay in beds, stood in windows, changed the colors of drapes!

And then, reinforcements.

From attic trapdoors, blind robot faces peered down with faucet mouths gushing green chemical.

The fire backed off, as even an elephant must at the sight of a dead snake. Now there were twenty snakes whipping over the floor, killing the fire with a clear cold venom of green froth.

But the fire was clever. It had sent flame outside the house, up through the attic to the pumps there. An explosion! The attic brain which directed the pumps was shattered into bronze shrapnel on the beams.

The fire rushed back into every closet and felt of the clothes hung there.

The house shuddered, oak bone on bone, its bared skeleton cringing from the heat, its wire, its nerves revealed as if a surgeon had torn the skin off to let the red veins and capillaries quiver in the scalded air. Help, help! Fire! Run, run! Heat snapped mirrors like the first brittle winter ice. And the voices wailed. Fire, fire, run, run, like a tragic nursery rhyme, a dozen voices, high, low, like children dying in a forest, alone, alone. And the voices fading as the wires popped their sheathings like hot chestnuts. One, two, three, four, five voices died.

In the nursery the jungle burned. Blue lions roared, purple giraffes bounded off. The panthers ran in circles, changing color, and ten million animals, running before the fire, vanished off toward a distant steaming river. . . .

Ten more voices died. In the last instant under the fire avalanche, other choruses, oblivious, could be heard announcing the time, playing music, cutting the lawn by remote-control mower, or setting an umbrella frantically out and in the slamming and opening front door, a thousand things happening, like a clock shop when each clock strikes the hour insanely before or after the other, a scene of maniac confusion, yet unity; singing, screaming, a few last cleaning mice darting bravely out to carry the horrid ashes away! And one voice, with sublime disregard for the situation, read poetry aloud in the fiery study, until all the film spools burned, until all the wires withered and the circuits cracked.

The fire burst the house and let it slam flat down, puffing out skirts of spark and smoke.

In the kitchen, an instant before the rain of fire and timber, the stove could be seen making breakfasts at a psychopathic rate, ten dozen eggs, six loaves of toast, twenty dozen bacon strips, which, eaten by fire, started the stove working again, hysterically hissing!

The crash. The attic smashing into kitchen and parlor. The parlor into cellar, cellar into sub-cellar. Deep freeze, armchair, film tapes, circuits, beds, and all like skeletons thrown in a cluttered mound deep under.

Smoke and silence. A great quantity of smoke.

Dawn showed faintly in the east. Among the ruins, one wall stood alone. Within the wall, a last voice said, over and over again and again, even as the sun rose to shine upon the heaped rubble and steam:

"Today is August 5, 2026, today is August 5, 2026, today is . . ."

BUILDING A WRITING CONTEXT

1. How do you think Ray Bradbury feels about technology?
2. In what ways does the house seem like a person?
3. The title of this story was taken from the title of the quoted poem by Sara Teasdale. Why do you think Bradbury used this poem in his story?

THE WRITING WORKSHOP

Preparing to Write

The first installment of *Superman* started with a drawing that showed the planet Krypton exploding, while a small rocket carried the infant Superman towards Earth and safety. Because of that one drawing, many people became hooked on astronomy, rocketry, and a type of literature called *science fiction*.

Science fiction is both the oldest and newest kind of literature. In fact, it is as old as dreaming. It will be forever new, because there will always be something to discover.

Science fantasy, speculative fiction, fantastic fiction, space fiction, speculative fantasy, scientific romance, SF, sci-fi . . . the labels and definitions of science fiction are many. In the past few years, science fiction has become one of the main literary streams of our time — one out of three novels sold today is science fiction.

However, it is difficult to arrive at a definition of SF which will satisfy all readers. One thing we can safely say — SF is a special sort of writing that makes use of fantastic or inventive elements to comment on society, humanity, life, the cosmos, and any other topic under the general heading of philosophy.

Developing the Writing

A. Read the following short story by Frederic Brown, reprinted here in its totality:
"After the last atomic war, Earth was dead; nothing grew, nothing lived. The last man sat in a room. There was a knock on the door. . ."
Finish the story.

B. Many science fiction stories deal with visitors from outer space. Do you think any of the following mysterious though well documented events has a connection with outer space? Write brief possible explanations for two of the events.

1. **The Golden Airplane**
   A pre-Columbian gold artifact from South America, made more than 1000 years ago, looks very much like the model of a delta-winged jet.

2. **Ezekiel's Wheel**
   The Old Testament prophet Ezekiel was exiled from Israel in 597 B.C. Five years later he had a "vision of God." An aerial chariot containing four-winged monsters and travelling on wheels within wheels arrived before him in a storm wind with flashes of fire.

3. **The Green Children**
   In August 1887, two children with bright-green skin and slanted eyes came out of a Spanish cave. They wore clothes made of a strange material, and spoke a language that experts from Barcelona were unable to identify.

4. **The Siberian Explosion**

   An explosion as powerful as a hydrogen bomb shook Siberia on June 30, 1908. There was nothing to account for it.

5. **The Hills' Visit to a Spaceship**

   On September 19, 1961, while driving through a deserted summer resort in New Hampshire, Betty and Barney Hill were stopped by a disk-shaped flying object and dragged into the craft. They were later released. Under hypnosis they remembered and were able to tell what had happened.

C. Choose one of the mysterious events described in Activity B above. Use it as the basis for a short science fiction story.

D. It's always worthwhile to remember that the first half of the term *science fiction* is *science*. Read through the following science topics and develop one of them into a short science fiction story.

1. Possibilities in plastics.
2. How atomic energy can be used for industrial purposes.
3. Advantages of frequency modulation.
4. A modern invention.
5. Travel in the next decade.
6. A recent development in medicine.
7. Vitamins.
8. Plastic surgery.
9. The house of tomorrow.
10. DDT builds super insects.
11. Fabrics of the future.
12. Future of the automobile.

Revising and Editing

Students often fail to present their written work as well as they are able because they have not learned proofreading skills. Mistakes in spelling, grammar, word usage, and statements of facts can often be corrected quite easily once you notice them. It is important to train yourself to look for such errors.

Gradually you will become more accurate, more confident, and quicker with your proofreading. Proofreading applies to all subject areas and types of written work — math, science, maps, charts, reports, stories, poems, dramas, and so on. Carefully proofread one or more pieces of writing you did in this chapter, making corrections as needed.

Growing from Writing

A. We have created machines that have tremendous capacity for duplicating human effort. How much of our work and thinking do you think we will want or be able to entrust to machines? Do you think we will get along better with machines than we have with each other? Use these questions as the basis for a class discussion.

B. Many science fiction novels and short stories deal with outer space. In order to become more aware of the many facets of space, write brief definitions for seven of the following. Use a dictionary and/or encyclopedia if you need help.

1. Asteroid.
2. Comet.
3. Meteor.
4. Planet.
5. Quasar.
6. Star.
7. Black hole.
8. Galaxy.
9. Nova.
10. Pulsar.
11. Satellite.
12. Supernova.

Now use at least two of the above terms in a short science fiction poem or story.

Mysteries

The Phantom Flag-Waver

Why do people love mysteries? Perhaps it's the desire to learn other people's secrets (and keep their own hidden!) As you unravel a mystery, you are using your abilities to think logically, to notice details, and to establish relationships between events. As a writer of a mystery story, you use the same processes.

The Railroad Ghost MURRAY T. PRINGLE

It was a spooky night. As the crack British express train raced through the chilly darkness, fog began to close in around it. It was just the sort of night anything could happen — a night one might even expect to meet a ghost.

Now running a train isn't easy any time, but on this particular evening it was really hard work. Fog pressed in on the speeding folds of velvet. Even with the powerful headlight stabbing the darkness ahead, the engineer had to strain his eyes to see the track.

He was very much annoyed at the fog, because today of all days he wanted to make a record run. And the reason was that Queen Victoria herself was among the several hundred passengers on the train.

Suddenly a horrified gasp escaped his lips. Dead ahead, and outlined in the brilliant beam of the engine's headlamp, a figure in a black cloak stood in the middle of the tracks waving its arms frantically! The engineer made a desperate grab for the brakes and brought the express to a screeching halt.

After quieting the excited and frightened passengers, the trainmen got out to investigate. They searched and called, but there was no sign of the mysterious figure who had flagged their train.

Who had he been, and why had he stopped the train? The crewmen were puzzled. They decided someone had been playing a joke. Even the engineer was almost convinced that it had either been somebody's poor idea of a joke or his imagination playing tricks. But he wasn't absolutely sure.

Just to make certain, he swung down from his cab and walked up the tracks. Suddenly his face grew pale and his heart beat wildly. There, a scant two hundred yards ahead of the stopped train, he found a washed-out bridge! The whole thing had toppled into a swollen stream. If it had not been for the mysterious flagman, the train would have plunged into the stream, killing passengers and crew.

While the bridge and tracks were being repaired, the train crew made another search, but they could not find the slightest trace of the strange figure who had saved the train.

Not until the train reached London safely was the mystery solved.

Lying at the base of the locomotive headlamp, the engineer found a huge dead moth. He held the insect in his hand and frowned thoughtfully.

Then he did a strange thing. He wet the wings of the moth and carefully pasted it to the glass of the headlamp. Then he climbed back into the cab of his engine and switched on the light.

"Ah!" he cried triumphantly. "I thought so!" For as the bright beam stabbed ahead into the darkness, there appeared once again the "phantom" the engineer had seen earlier. But now the "arms" weren't waving wildly. They were still.

The mysterious rescuer had been this huge moth! Somehow in the few seconds before the train reached the wrecked bridge, it had flown into the beam of the headlight. And because in the dense fog the trapped insect had resembled a cloaked figure waving its arms, many people — including the Queen of England herself — had been saved!

Did this really happen? Well, if you're ever in London, go to the Museum of Natural History and ask to see the "Victoria Moth." You will be shown a huge moth in a glass case — the moth the British call the Phantom Flagman!

BUILDING A WRITING CONTEXT

1. **When did you suspect the solution to the mystery?**
2. **What elements does this story have in common with other mysteries?**
3. **This story was based on an actual event. What other *factual* mystery stories have you heard or read?**
4. **What is your favorite *fictional* mystery story? Why?**

THE WRITING WORKSHOP

Preparing to Write

Mystery writers attempt to make us curious — not just about "who did it" but "why they did it" and "how it was done." We begin to understand that the way in which people behave is determined by motives — the reasons behind their actions.

Most people like to outwit others. Writing a mystery story gives you a chance to control the situation, to invent motives, to give clues, and to design obstacles — all in order to challenge your reader's imagination.

Developing the Writing

A. Create a *motive circle*. In the middle of a sheet of paper, write the name of a crime such as purse snatching. Then create a web of the motives that could have led up to the crime in the center. How many different motives can you list?

B. You are a witness for the police and are viewing suspected people in a line-up. Describe the faces you see through the one-way mirror.

C. Use ideas from Activities A and B above to write a mystery story centering on a crime and how it was solved.

D. You have been found at the scene of a crime that you did not commit, but for which you are arrested. What happens when your parents come to the police station, and how do you prove your innocence? Write the story.

E. Not all mystery stories involve crime. For instance, some are about ghosts or hidden treasure or strange disappearances. Write a mystery story about a topic other than crime. As an example, refer back to the story "The Railroad Ghost."

Revising and Editing

Work with a classmate. Read one of your mystery stories aloud. What questions does your partner have that will help you create a clearer picture? What details can you add to or delete from your story?

Should you delay the ending or add some tensions along the way to heighten suspense? Have you given suitable motives to the characters who carried out the actions in the story?

Improve your story in any way you can.

Sharing and Publishing

Read only half of your mystery story to a group of classmates or to the whole class. Have them predict how your story will end.

- How close were their guesses?
- How could you fool your readers into expecting one ending, and then surprise them with another?

Growing from Writing

A. **Keeping a Journal**

Jot down in your journal three personal mysteries in your life. They could be either mysteries that you would like to solve, or that probably have no solutions until life is completed. These personal mysteries can be the basis for a free-verse poem that explores your own problems in a private way.

B. Survey the covers of mystery novels in the library or a book store. What elements do they all have in common? Which novels might you consider reading? Why?

C. For this Activity, the class is divided into small groups. Each group works in a different part of the room so that one group cannot see what another is doing.

Each group works with a different set of five objects. Each member of a group picks one of the objects, examines it carefully without touching it, and writes a description so that a student from another group could pick out the object by feel alone.

When everyone is finished writing, the objects are covered. While other groups watch, one group at a time comes to a table. One student at a time is blindfolded, hears one description read, and tries to pick the object by touch alone.

You can then discuss how successful the description was. Accurate description is often a key element of a good mystery story. How could you improve the description in one or more mystery stories written in this chapter? Do it.

Personal Reactions

The Laughing One

Emily Carr was born in Victoria in 1871. Her unique paintings and writings were inspired by her surroundings. West coast forest settings and the life of the Native peoples make up much of the subject matter. Carr is considered a major figure in the development of Canadian art. Her nickname, Klee Wyck ("the laughing one"), was given by the Coastal Native people, and offers insight into her character. She died in 1945.

Klee Wyck was a truly great artist. Her devotion to Canada marked everything she did. She approached no subject in writing or in painting in a purely self-centered way. She was driven always by a passion to make her own experiences vivid and real for the onlooker or reader.

Sleep EMILY CARR

When I was a child I was staying at one of Victoria's beaches.

I was down on the point watching a school of porpoises at play off Trail Island when a canoe came round the headland. She was steering straight for our beach. . . .

In the canoe were a man and woman, half a dozen children, a dog, a cat and a coop of fowls, besides all the Indians' things. She was a West Coast canoe — dug out of a great red cedar tree. She was long and slim, with a high prow shaped like a wolf's head. She was painted black with a line of blue running round the top of the inside. Her stern went straight down into the water. The Indian mother sat in the stern and steered the canoe with a paddle.

When the canoe was near the shore, the man and the woman drove their paddles strong and hard, and the canoe shot high up onto the pebbles with a growling sound. The barefoot children swarmed over her side and waded.

The man and the woman got out and dragged the canoe high onto the beach. There was a baby tucked into the woman's shawl; the shawl bound the child close to her body. She waddled slowly across the beach, her bare feet settling in the sand with every step, her fleshy body squared down onto her feet. All the movements of the man and the woman were slow and steady; their springless feet padded flatly; their backs and shoulders were straight. The few words they said to each other were guttural and low-pitched.

The Indian children did not race up and down the beach, astonished at strange new things, as we always were. These children belonged to the beach, and were as much a part of it as the drift-logs and the stones.

The man gathered a handful of sticks and lit a fire. They took a big iron pot and their food out of the canoe, and set them by the fire. The woman sat among the things with her baby — she managed the shawl and the baby so that she had her arms free, and her hands moved among the kettles and food.

The man and a boy, about as big as I was, came up the path on the bank with tin pails. When they saw me, the boy hung back and stared. The man grinned and pointed to our well. He had coarse hair hanging to his shoulders; it was unbrushed and his head was bound with a red band. He had wrinkles everywhere, face, hands and clothing. His coat and pants were in tatters. He was brown and dirty all over, but his face was gentle and kind.

Soon I heard the pad-pad of their naked feet on the clay of the path. The water from the boy's pail slopped in the dust while he stared back at me.

They made tea and ate stuff out of the iron pot; it was fish, I could smell it. The man and the woman sat beside the pot, but the children took pieces and ran up and down eating them.

They had hung a tent from the limb of the old willow tree that lolled over the sand from the bank. The bundles and blankets had been tossed into the tent; the flaps were open and I could see everything lying higgledy-piggledy inside.

Each child ate what he wanted, then he went into the tent

and tumbled, dead with sleep, among the bundles. The man, too, stopped eating and went into the tent and lay down. The dog and the cat were curled up among the blankets.

The woman on the beach drew the smouldering logs apart; when she poured a little water on them they hissed. Last of all she too went into the tent with her baby.

The tent full of sleep greyed itself into the shadow under the willow tree. The wolf's head of the canoe stuck up black on the beach a little longer; then it faded back and back into the night. The sea kept on going slap-slap-slap over the beach.

BUILDING A WRITING CONTEXT

1. **Emily Carr often wrote about her experiences. This article does not have a plot leading to a climax. Instead, it recreates a memorable experience. Why do you think Emily Carr remembered this incident from her childhood?**
2. **"These children belonged to the beach, and were as much a part of it as the drift-logs and the stones." Discuss this statement in relation to the theme of "home" or "roots."**

THE WRITING WORKSHOP

Preparing to Write

The following assignments are intended to help you:
- Find a "voice" in writing.
- Build a feeling of confidence that you "can" write.

Start with what you know and feel — in your own words.

Developing the Writing

A. The purpose of this assignment is to encourage you to use your most easily available resource — yourself — as the source of material for narrative writing. Concentrate on capturing the particular detail and feeling of each incident as you do the assignment. Do not be concerned with gramatically perfect or complete narratives at this time.

You will be asked to go back in time to capture four incidents in your life. Each incident may be important or trivial, but it should be one that stands out in your mind. Record it in writing. Be brief but at the same time make the incident as real as you can.

1. Go back in time 24 hours. Remember one incident from yesterday. Record it in writing.
2. Go back in time a week and remember something you were doing on this day seven days ago. Record it in writing.
3. Go back a year. Record in writing an incident you remember from about this same time last year.
4. Now concentrate really hard and go back as far as you can. Record you first "clear" memory.

Choose one of the four incidents you briefly recorded. Expand it into a "personal reaction" article. If you wish, use "Sleep" by Emily Carr as a model. This time, pay attention to completeness, grammar, punctuation, and spelling.

B. Pretend you are an artist painting your masterpiece, the painting that will make you famous for generations to come. What does the painting show? Describe it in a short personal note.

C. Look back into your memory. Compare a person or place as they were in the past with your perception of the same person or place now. Write in the form of a short personal article that could be published in a newspaper or magazine.

Revising and Editing

In revising your article, watch especially for the following sentence errors.

- Sentence fragments.
- Run-on sentences.
- Lack of sentence variety (for example, too many short, choppy sentences or too many long, complicated ones).

Sharing and Publishing

You probably do your best writing when the result is to be presented or published in some way. Choose one piece of writing done in this chapter. Polish it, making it as good as you can. Share it with others in one of the following ways:

- Put it up on a bulletin board.

- Submit it to your school newspaper or another newspaper, or to a magazine, for possible publication.
- Include it with a letter that you send to a friend or relative. Ask the person who receives it to respond to your ideas as expressed in the article.

Growing from Writing

Look for books and paintings by Emily Carr. Find out why and how she became both a famous painter and writer. What can you learn from Emily Carr's life that you could apply to your own life?

Friendly Letters

My Dear Gertrude

"It is not often that someone comes along who is a true friend and a good writer." E.B. White in *Charlotte's Web*

One medium of writing that allows you to be both a good friend and a good writer is the friendly letter. Friendly letters (also called personal or social letters) account for the largest part of the 100 billion pieces of mail handled annually by North American post offices.

The first letter below is a modern example, written by a student. The second is a letter from author Lewis Carroll to a child friend, written over 100 years ago.

27 Marmot Avenue
Spruce Grove, Kansas
19788
May 26, 1986

Dear Tiffany,

As you probably know, my birthday is coming up in two weeks, and I was wondering if you would like to come. The party will start at about 5:00 p.m. on June 13, and it will end at about 1:00 p.m. on June 14. Yes, it is a sleepover!

You should bring a sleeping bag and a pillow and, if you can, a flashlight. We will be sleeping in our camping trailer, so maybe you should bring some extra warm pajamas!

My friends are really looking forward to meeting you, so I hope you can come. I'm sure that you will like my friends. They are really nice! Write back soon.

Sincerely,
Sheila Cameron

Christ Church, Oxford,
October 13th, 1875.

My dear Gertrude,

I never give birthday *presents*, but you see I *do* sometimes write a birthday *letter*: so, as I've just arrived here, I am writing this to wish you many and many a happy return of your birthday to-morrow. I will drink your health if only I can remember, and if you don't mind — but perhaps you object?

You see, if I were to sit by you at breakfast, and to drink your tea, you wouldn't like that, would you? You would say, "Boo! hoo! Here's Mr. Dodgson drunk my tea, and I haven't got any left!" So I am very much afraid, next time Sybil looks for you, she'll find you sitting by the sad seawaves and crying, "Boo! hoo! Here's Mr. Dodgson has drunk my health and I haven't got any left!"

And how it will puzzle Mr. Maund, when he is sent for to see you! "My dear madam, I'm sorry to say your little girl has got no health at all! I never saw such a thing in my life!" "You see, she would go and make friends with a strange gentleman, and yesterday he drank her health!" "Well, Mrs. Chataway," he will say, "the only way to cure her is to wait till his next birthday, and then for *her* to drink his health."

And then we shall have changed healths. I wonder how you'll like mine! Oh, Gertrude, I wish you would not talk such nonsense!

Your loving friend,
Lewis Carroll.

BUILDING A WRITING CONTEXT

1. **Both letters deal with birthdays. However, the letter-writers' purposes differed. What was the first letter-writer's purpose in writing? What was the second letter-writer's purpose?**
2. **Why are the return address and date given at the top of a letter? What differences in punctuation do you notice between the two letters above? The letter from Sheila Cameron uses *open punctuation.* The letter from Lewis Carroll uses *closed punctuation.* Either is acceptable, but**

the style must be the same throughout the letter and also on the envelope.

3. The words *Sincerely* and *Your loving friend* are known as *complimentary closings*. What punctuation follows each? List four other complimentary closings commonly used in friendly letters.

THE WRITING WORKSHOP

Preparing to Write

What are the occasions for most friendly letters? They include the following.

- News. Somebody, somewhere, today, would like to know what you and your family have been doing, thinking, planning, talking about.
- Love. (Define this one for yourself!)
- Thanks. Someone has given you a present, done you a favor, or entertained you. Courtesy calls for a letter of appreciation.
- Invitations and replies. Although many informal invitations today are just telephoned, and some formal ones are engraved, on many occasions a written invitation is most suitable. Replies to written or engraved invitations are also often written.
- Best wishes and congratulations. A note just before a holiday season or a birthday shows much more personal interest than a printed card does. And if a friend of yours has done anything especially noteworthy, a letter will help show how happy you are about your friend's happiness.
- Get well soon. If a friend is hospitalized or seriously ill at home, a personal note will help cheer him or her.
- Apology. You may have made an unpleasant mistake — lost your temper, broken somebody's valuable candle-holder, or something similar. A simple letter of apology will make both you and the other person feel better.
- Sympathy. The hardest letter to write, one of sympathy, is called for when a friend is bereaved. One of the main things to say, of course, is that you are thinking of your friend in the time of his or her sorrow.

For friendly letters, stationery should be of good quality, with matching envelopes. Ink is usually blue or black; watery colors or very bright colors should be avoided. Typing is now considered permissible, but is normally avoided in invitations, replies, notes of sympathy, and other short notes in which a highly personal touch is desirable.

The language of any friendly letter should be as appropriate to the receiver as the content is. If you are writing to someone with whom you would talk in slang, use that kind of language. If you are writing to an adult, your language will probably be rather different.

Developing the Writing

A. Choose a friend, real or imaginary. Write him or her a letter based on one of the following situations.

1. You are returning a book or some other object that you borrowed from a friend. Write a letter thanking him or her for lending it to you.
2. You had arranged to meet a friend in town, but it was quite impossible for you to be there. Explain why you were not able to meet him or her. Apologize for the inconvenience you may have caused and suggest another meeting.
3. Write a letter to a "pen pal" in another country.
4. Write a letter to a friend, giving him or her advice on what to take along on a camping holiday.

B. Choose a relative, real or imaginary. Write him or her a letter based on one of the following situations.

1. You have just returned home after a pleasant visit to a relative. Write a letter thanking this relative for his or her hospitality and saying what you enjoyed most while you were there.
2. You have just heard that a relative of yours has had an accident and is in hospital. Write a letter wishing him or her a speedy recovery.
3. You received a present of some money from a relative. Write a letter thanking this relative for the present and saying what you intend to do with it.
4. Write a letter to a relative who has written to you complaining that you never write.

C. Write a letter based on one of the following situations.

1. You have been invited to a party. Write a letter accepting the

invitation and inquiring if it would be appropriate for you to bring a friend or relative with you.

2. Write a letter refusing an invitation to a party and explaining why you cannot go.

Revising and Editing

A. Use the following questions to check your letters for surface errors.

1. Did I put my return address and the date at the top?
2. Did I use an appropriate salutation? (Examples: Dear Mary, Dear Uncle Fred.)
3. Did I double-check the spelling of all words I was unsure about?
4. Did I leave wide margins so that my writing was uncrowded and easy to read?
5. Did I indent each new paragraph?
6. Did the punctuation I used make the meaning clear?
7. Did I capitalize names and titles, and the first word of each sentence?
8. Did I use a variety of sentence types?
9. Did I use complete sentences where necessary?
10. Did I use clear handwriting that would be easy to read?
11. Did I finish with a suitable complimentary closing before my signature? Examples: *Yours truly, Love, Your affectionate grandson, As ever.*

B. Write final drafts of one or more letters that you wrote in this chapter.

Sharing and Publishing

Consider actually mailing final drafts of one or more of your letters.

Growing from Writing

Letters can be important as literature and/or as first-hand sources of information about the past. Read excerpts from one or more of the following, or from similar books.

- *The Life and Letters of Lewis Carroll*, published by The Century Company.

- *West Coast Chinese Boy* by Sing Lim.
- *Affectionately Yours* (letters of John A. Macdonald and his family), edited by J.K. Johnson.
- Letters of St. Paul (found in the Bible).
- *The Screwtape Letters* by C.S. Lewis.
- *Letters from Carrie* by Janet Harder.
- *Letters to Horseface: Being the Story of Wolfgang Amadeus Mozart's Journey to Italy, 1769-1770, When He Was a Boy of Fourteen* by F.N. Monjo.
- *Letters from a Lady Rancher* by Monica Hopkins.

Report back to the class on what you have read. Your report may be either oral or written.

Descriptive Paragraphs

Wilderness Boy

Usually a *paragraph* is a group of sentences telling about one idea or event. The idea or event told about is called the *topic.*

There are several kinds of paragraphs.

- **A *descriptive paragraph* presents a word picture of a person, thing, place, or event — or some aspect of one of these.**
- **A *narrative paragraph* tells a story or part of a story.**
- **An *expository paragraph* explains something.**

Many paragraphs are actually a combination of two or even three different kinds. For instance, a descriptive paragraph might also tell a story to some extent.

from Two Against the North FARLEY MOWAT

In appearance Awasin was Jamie's opposite. He was lean as a whip, with long black hair that hung almost to his shoulders. His eyes too were black, and they smiled as often as his mouth — and that was very often. For three seasons Awasin had attended the Indian school in far-off Pelican Narrows, so that he could read and speak English almost as well as any city boy. But most of his life had been lived in the heart of the forests and the wilderness was as much a part of him as his own skin.

The current sucked at his trembling legs. He lost his balance as he reached for the canoe. One hand clutched the broken gunwale of the vessel, and he dragged himself up to it. From then on it was a struggle of sheer will power against the brute power of the river. In a daze he fought, inch by inch, toward the shore while the water-logged canoe tugged and hauled away from him. Several times he lost his foothold and both he and the canoe swung back toward the fatal journey. Each time he managed to arrest the progress in the nick of time. At last he felt the canoe grate against the shore. Dizziness overwhelmed him. He stumbled forward on his knees — and fainted dead away.

Getting to the Graduation Party

It is easy to get to Angelo's house. Follow James Street past the stadium parking lot. Take the first left to Westdale High School. Then watch for the Burger King on the corner of Mohawk and Brant. Next, turn right onto Brant and continue over the railroad tracks. When you see the Texaco station on the right, look for Ellis Avenue. Turn left onto Ellis. Angelo and the graduation party are at 33 Ellis.

BUILDING A WRITING CONTEXT

1. **State the topic of each paragraph above.**
2. **Which paragraph is mostly descriptive? Mostly narrative? Mostly expository?**
3. **Descriptive paragraphs often make effective use of adjectives and adverbs. Discuss the use of these in the descriptive paragraph above.**

THE WRITING WORKSHOP

Preparing to Write

A. Effective paragraphs often have these three parts:

- The topic sentence usually states the topic of the paragraph and gives the reader some idea of what the writer intends to say.
- The developing sentences provide more information about the topic.
- The closing sentence often summarizes the paragraph and/or makes a striking comment about the topic.

B. In this chapter you will be writing descriptive paragraphs. To write effective descriptions, writers should make effective use of adjectives, adverbs, and comparisons. They should try to appeal to as many senses as possible.

As a topic, select one member of your family to describe. Read again the description of Awasin, noting how Farley Mowat describes this character in his book *Two Against the North.*

Developing the Writing

Begin by developing a thought web something like the following.

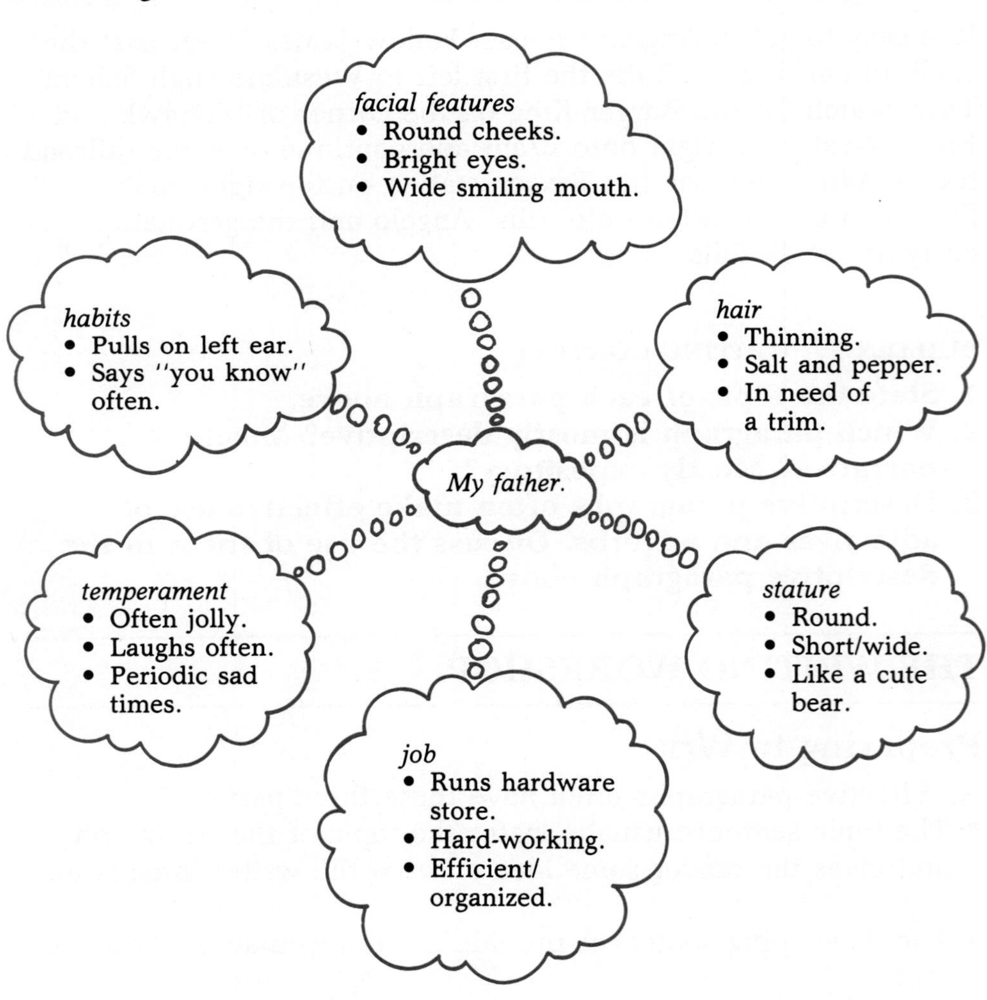

Now plan your paragraph using ideas from the thought web. Remember that your main aim is to describe, not to tell a story. In your notebook complete the writing plan below:

Topic: ____________________

Ideas for an opening sentence: ____________________

____

Ideas for developmental sentences: ____________________

____

____

____

Ideas for a closing sentence: ____________________

____

Using your plan, write the first draft of your paragraph.

Revising and Editing

A. Revise your paragraph using the checklist below.

1. Did I write an effective opening sentence?
2. Is my topic clear to the reader?
3. Do all of my developmental sentences provide more information about the topic?
4. Did I write a good closing sentence?
5. Did I write my sentences in a logical order?
6. Did I use descriptive words and comparisons effectively?
7. Did I appeal to the senses of hearing, sight, smell, touch, and/or taste to involve my readers and bring my description to life?

B. With a writing partner, now proofread your paragraph, using the questions below.

1. Does each sentence make sense?
2. Have I used capital letters correctly?
3. Have I punctuated each sentence properly?
4. Did I spell words correctly, checking those I was unsure about?
5. Did I use proper form with regard to indenting and margins?
6. Is my handwriting clear and easy to read?

Sharing and Publishing

A. Prepare a bulletin board display of your class's descriptive paragraphs. You could, in some cases, include photographs of the family members being described.

B. Publish your paragraph as part of a greeting card to be sent to the family member described. It can be sent any time, but you may wish to wait until Mother's Day, a birthday, Christmas, or some other special day.

Growing from Writing

A. Look through a copy of your local newspaper to locate good examples of paragraphs that are:

- Mostly descriptive.
- Mostly narrative.
- Mostly expository.

Clip the two best paragraphs in each category that you can find. Then work with two other students who have done the same thing. Read your samples aloud and discuss them. First, talk about why you classed them as you did. Next, talk about why you think they are good examples of that type of paragraph.

B. Focus on the main image in your descriptive paragraph. Rewrite it in the form of a haiku poem.

Journals

Anne Alive

Have you ever written an important note to yourself on a scrap of paper, and then lost the paper? It is important to many people to write down ideas, facts, observations, and feelings. Instead of doing this in a disorganized fashion, many people — including sea captains, writers, and police officers — keep journals or logs.

A journal is a record, an entry-book kept regularly, though not necessarily daily. It is a record kept for oneself. As such, it may be disjointed and uneven in quality. It is not meant to be polished.

A good example of a journal is *The Diary of Anne Frank*. Anne Frank was a Jewish girl living in Holland during the Nazi occupation of World War II. To escape being sent to concentration camps, it was necessary for many Jews to hide. Anne and her family went into hiding on July 5, 1942, in a group of rooms joined to a warehouse.

The first three journal entries given below were written before Anne and her family went into hiding. In her journal Anne often wrote to an imaginary friend, whom she called Kitty.

from The Diary of Anne Frank

Monday, 15 June, 1942

I had my birthday party on Sunday afternoon. We showed a film *The Lighthouse Keeper* with Rin-Tin-Tin, which my school friends thoroughly enjoyed. We had a lovely time. There were lots of girls and boys. Mummy always wants to know whom I'm going to marry. . . .

Saturday, 20 June, 1942

I haven't written for a few days, because I wanted first of all to think about my diary. It's an odd idea for someone like me to keep a diary; not only because I have never done so before, but because it seems to me that neither I — nor for that matter anyone else — will be interested in the unbosomings of a thirteen-year-old schoolgirl. Still, what does that matter? I want to write, but more than that, I want to bring out all kinds of things that lie buried deep in my heart. . . .

Wednesday, 8 July, 1942

Dear Kitty,
Years seem to have passed between Sunday and now. So much has happened, it is just as if the whole world had turned upside down. But I am still alive, Kitty, and that is the main thing, Daddy says.

Yes, I'm still alive, indeed, but don't ask where or how. You wouldn't understand a word, so I will begin by telling you what happened on Sunday afternoon.

At three o'clock (Harry had just gone, but was coming back later) someone rang the front doorbell. I was lying lazily reading a book on the veranda in the sunshine, so I didn't hear it. A bit later, Margot appeared at the kitchen door looking very excited. "The S.S. have sent a call-up notice for Daddy," she whispered. "Mummy has gone to see Mr. Van Daan already." (Van Daan is a friend who works with Daddy in the business.) It was a great shock to me, a call-up; everyone knows what that means. I picture concentration camps and lonely cells — should we allow him to be doomed to this? "Of course he won't go," declared Margot, while we waited together. "Mummy has gone to the Van Daans to discuss whether we should move into our hiding place tomorrow. . . ."

Thursday, 9 July, 1942

Dear Kitty,
So we walked in the pouring rain, Daddy, Mummy, and I, each with a school satchel and shopping bag filled to the brim with all kinds of things thrown together anyhow.

We got sympathetic looks from people on their way to work. You could see by their faces how sorry they were they couldn't offer us a lift; the gaudy yellow star spoke for itself.

Only when we were on the road did Mummy and Daddy begin to tell me bits and pieces about the plan. For months as many of our goods and chattels and necessities of life as possible had been sent away and they were sufficiently ready for us to have gone into hiding of our own accord on July 16. The plan had had to be speeded up ten days because of the call-up, so our quarters would not be so well organized, but we had to make the best of it. The hiding place itself would be in the building where Daddy has his office. . . .

Friday, 21 August, 1942

Dear Kitty,
The entrance to our hiding place has now been properly concealed. Mr. Kraler thought it would be better to put a cupboard in front our door (because a lot of houses are being searched for hidden bicycles), but of course it had to be a movable cupboard that can open like a door.

Mr. Vossen made the whole thing. We had already let him into the secret and he can't do enough to help. If we want to go downstairs, we have to first bend down and then jump, because the step has gone. The first three days we were all going about with masses of lumps on our foreheads, because we all knocked ourselves against the low doorway. Now we have nailed a cloth filled with wood wool against the top of the door. Let's see if that helps!

BUILDING A WRITING CONTEXT

1. A journal is often a record of everyday events. What everyday events did Anne tell of in her journal?

2. A journal is a place to write about strong feelings. What feelings did Anne record?

3. **In what ways was Anne's life similar to yours? How was it different?**
4. **State one thing you learned about Anne's personality through reading these journal entries?**

THE WRITING WORKSHOP

Preparing to Write

A. A journal entry is not only a record *for* oneself, but also *of* oneself. A journal may be many things.

- Think of your journal as a tape-recorder attached directly to your brain. Sometimes you can simply record your stream-of-consciousness thoughts. Don't fuss about exact words; simply write as fast as you think.
- Think of your journal as a storehouse into which you pack goods for a rainy day, when you can browse through with nostalgia and amazement.
- Think of your journal as a laboratory for experiments — blank pages waiting to be tried. Ask questions, and set about finding answers.
- Think of your journal as a treasury for quotes, ideas, puns, impressions, and mental images.
- Think of your journal as a letter to yourself. What would you have yourself know? Or what would you like to remember ten years from now?
- Think of your journal as an excellent way to do pre-writing for assignments. Save ideas you pick up from films, people, books, pictures, music, and television. Record them in your journal. Interesting words or phrases can be saved there as well. If you observe something of interest, write it in your journal before you forget it. Such ideas, words, etc. can be used later to get you started on a piece of writing.

B. **Two Important Reasons for Journal-Writing**

- One important value of journal writing is that you can write freely without fear of having your writing judged.
- The very act of writing helps to clarify ideas.

C. **Where Is My Journal?**

Consider these possibilities:

- In a bound journal book or diary.

- In a special notebook.
- In a separate section of my language arts notebook.

D. **When Do I Write in My Journal?**

- Whenever you want to save a good idea or an interesting phrase for a later time.
- Whenever you want to express how you feel about something.
- As a regular part of language arts period.
- At a set time in class each day.
- As the last thing you do before you go to bed.

Developing the Writing

A. One way to learn to use your journal well is to write specific kinds of information in it for certain periods of time. You might follow the pattern below:

- *Week One*
  Write down two or three interesting or unusual events each day.

- *Week Two*
  Write down how you feel at several different times of the day for seven days.

- *Week Three*
  List interesting words and phrases you read or hear during the week.

- *Week Four*
  Use your journal to express your own ideas about specific questions of interest to you.
  Example: Is there life beyond Earth?

B. During other periods you might write in your journal on particular topics such as:

- My experience with death.
- My hopes for the future.
- Mistakes I would like to forget.
- People I respect.
- Some of my problems.
- What I like about my friends.
- People make me angry when. . . .

Sharing and Publishing

We may wish our journals to be read only by those closest to us, and then only with our permission. From time to time, try sharing portions of your journal with important people in your life, such as friends and family members.

Growing from Writing

A. It has been said that keeping a journal is in some ways like putting money in the bank. In a paragraph explain this statement.

B. Find the book *The Diary of Anne Frank*, and read more of Anne's story.

C. You have made a good start on your journal writing. Now, keep up the good work. If you write frequently in your journal, you will soon have a whole book. One day you will be able to pull an old journal from your shelf and delight in your ideas and feelings of years gone by.

Announcements

Medusa Is Only a Distant Cousin

Do you ever feel like making an announcement to the world about your frustrations? Each day you hear announcements made on television, over public address systems, and in newspapers. Usually they are issued in formal language by someone in authority. The following, however, are personal announcements.

Press Release
Susan Schweik, Student

miss schweik wishes to make it known to her
admiring public
that the rumor being spread saying in effect that
her hair is actually a sucking crawling
mass of snakes is
obviously false:
  in truth there was only one snake
  and it has been cosmetically removed.

to settle here and now the gossip,
medusa is only a distant cousin,
and not her sister as reported.

(besides, it wasn't poisonous).
so there.

An Announcement
Mary Long, Student

This is your last warning!
If you continue to ignore me,
If you continue to show no interest
in learning my name,
If you have not spoken a phrase of some sort to me
by the end of next week —
I will stop dreaming about you.
The Great American Novel
now being formulated in my head,
of which you are the central character,
will be terminated!
I've given you ample, fair, silent warning.
I await your actions.

Mean Song
Eve Merriam

Snickles and podes,
Ribble and grodes:
That's what I wish you.

A nox in the groot,
A root in the stoot
And a gock in the forebeshaw, too.

Keep out of sight
For fear that I might
Glom you a gravely snave.

Don't show your face
Around any place
Or you'll get one flack snack in the bave.

BUILDING A WRITING CONTEXT

1. **What kinds of people do you think are making these announcements?**
2. **Who do you think is the audience for each announcement?**

3. What personal announcement would you like to make — if you knew for sure that the right person or persons would pay attention to it?

THE WRITING WORKSHOP

Preparing to Write

When we open a newspaper, we often see birth announcements, death announcements, announcements of sales, of heroic deeds, of marriage, of entertainment, of prizes or competitions being won. Similarly we hear announcements made by friends, members of our families, the school broadcast system, the radio, and the TV set.

Before you write an announcement, you should decide:
- What information needs to be included.
- Why the announcement is being made.
- How you want your audience to respond to the announcement.

Developing the Writing

A. Write an announcement relating to one of the following situations in your life.
- Your own birth.
- Your winning of a contest or competition.
- A most important event in your life — past, present, or future.

B. By making an announcement about a fairly everyday happening, we can give the event significance. Write an announcement about one of the following.
- Cleaning your room.
- Preparing a meal.
- Getting your homework done.
- Cleaning out your locker.

C. If you are frustrated about something or have a complaint to make, you could make an announcement to voice your opinion. Write an announcement directed to one of the following people. You may wish to write in the form of a poem or letter.
- Teacher.
- Brother/sister.
- Prime Minister.
- World.

Revising and Editing

A. When you are trying to make a point, it is good practice to back up your statement so that your argument is stronger.

For example, if you are announcing to your family that you are treated unfairly, you can strengthen your point by providing evidence:

To My Family:
I am treated unfairly!
(Now add two items to help prove your point.)
1. ____________________
2. ____________________

Choose one of your announcements. Make it stronger and more specific by adding examples wherever possible.

B. Another editing technique is to make the same statement in more than one way. For example, you could say:

To My Family:
I am treated unfairly!
No one seems to care about my feelings!
Why don't you notice me? I count too!

By restating your point, you begin to demonstrate more than one reason for your feelings, and your position may become clearer.

Choose one of your announcements. Develop your position more strongly by restating your thoughts in at least two other ways.

Sharing and Publishing

Choose one of your announcements and present it publicly in one of the following ways.

1. Write it as a poster to be placed in a public place.
2. Prepare it as an oral reading. Choose your own role carefully and decide who your audience could role-play as they listen. (Will you ask people to respond after having heard your announcement?)

Growing from Writing

A. Create an announcement that you think might change the course of the world. This announcement could be about a great discovery, an invention, a natural disaster, a death, or similar event.

B. Think of an evil character from a story that you read when you were little; for example, The Big Bad Wolf or The Wicked Witch of the North. Create an announcement that would warn others about this character. What bad things has this person done? How can the person be recognized? What should one beware of?

Articles

Loch Ness Monster, Eat Your Heart Out

Every newspaper includes researched articles about topics of interest. Articles can be both informative and amusing.

New Dragon Will Surface This Month

HALIFAX *Chronicle-Herald/Mail-Star*

The monster of Loch Ness is in serious danger of being edged out of the limelight by Halifax County's Miller's Lake Dragon.

The 25-year-old resident of Miller's Lake has been receiving a lot of publicity over the past year and there will probably be a great deal more when the new dragon surfaces sometime this month.

The new dragon, which is made from fiberglass and metal rods, is replacing the original wooden serpent. The new dragon is structured so it will pose a menace to any would-be thieves.

Patty-Jean Snow, daughter of District 14 Councillor Gordon Snow, has designed the dragon to resemble a friendly Walt Disney character. Councillor Snow says he is amazed at the amount of interest that has been shown in the dragon and its history.

The dragon lived in relative obscurity until it disappeared last August. After a tremendous public outcry along with the promise of $100 reward the dragon was returned to its haunt. It joined a baby dragon that had been erected in its absence. The two cohabited happily for only a few months when thieves made off with the dragon's head permanently in December.

CBC has instituted a Miller's Lake Dragon Protection Association and the new dragon is hoping to enjoy a lengthy stay in Miller's Lake.

BUILDING A WRITING CONTEXT

1. How does the article's title attract the reader's interest?
2. What is the tone of the article?
3. How do you think the reporter researched the article?

THE WRITING WORKSHOP

Preparing to Write

When writing an article, you are concerned with exploring an interesting topic. First you should find all the information you can. Then you put this information into a form that people can read easily, understand, and enjoy. While you may be using some of your own ideas in writing the article, basically your task is to make researched information accessible to readers.

Developing the Writing

1. Work alone, with a partner, or with a group. Begin by choosing a topic of interest to you. The following general subjects may give you some ideas.
   - Problems of adolescence.
   - Difficulties with parents.
   - Life in the city/country.
   - Teenagers and advertising.
   - The fashion industry.
   - The impact of cars on how people live.
   - Computers.
   - The environment.
   - Consumerism.

2. Collect your information. If you are working with a partner or group, you can decide which part of the topic each person will research. Information can come from:
   - Interviews (in person or by phone).

- Newspapers (try to look at two or more different articles).
- Reference books (find the newest ones available).
- Government agencies (they publish many documents, which you can often obtain free just by asking).
- Your own observations (try to examine your experiences in an open-minded way).

3. Now organize your information. The following outline may help you plan your article.

   Title of Article: ____________________
   Opening (you could use an interesting little story, quotation, or statistic): ____________________
   ____

   First Major Point: ____________________
   a. (Information and Details) ____________________
   b. ____________________
   c. ____________________

   Second Major Point: ____________________
   a. (Information and Details) ____________________
   b. ____________________
   c. ____________________

   Third Major Point: ____________________
   a. (Information and Details) ____________________
   b. ____________________
   c. ____________________

   Conclusion (you could sum up your article, use another quotation, and/or make an important point that you have saved for the ending): ____________________
   ____

4. Write your article. If you are working with others, different people could write different sections of the article. Then you should all get together and make whatever changes are needed so that the whole article flows along smoothly and logically.

Revising and Editing

Proofread your article using the checklist on page 146.

Sharing and Publishing

Collect your articles into a class newspaper, or exchange them between groups. A good article will cause people to respond. You could attach a response page to each article, so that those who read it will be able to write down their views about it. The article's author or authors should then take a second look at the article, making improvements based on the response-page comments.

Growing from Writing

A. Build a classroom anthology of newspaper and magazine articles that speak especially to your generation. Use these articles as examples for your own writing.

B. Rewrite one of your articles as a letter to the editor. Attempt to have it published in a local newspaper.

Surveys and Articles

Counting Your Chicken Chunks

Some experts feel that soon half of the money spent on food will be eaten out of the home. Do you think this will be true for your community? Why or why not?
What is your favorite fast food? The following article discusses the popularity of chicken as a fast food.

With a Little Bit of Pluck

MARY HALEY, *St. Petersburg Times*

A chicken nugget by any other name is still stiff competition for McNugget pioneer McDonald's.

Competitors are dropping the "Mc" or calling their chicken products "chunks," but their commercials are aimed at cashing in on the popularity of McDonald's Chicken McNuggets. Church's Fried Chicken pushes its two types of chicken nuggets, regular and spicy, with ads featuring a Ronald McDonald look-alike clown wearing sunglasses. Kentucky Fried Chicken invites viewers to "know your nuggets" in a commercial introducing its chicken item.

Finger food products such as chicken nuggets are an increasingly popular choice among all age groups, according to Bruce Baird, marketing and retail director for Tyson Foods Inc. . . .

"If you look at the frozen foods market, there are several visible trends," he said. "People are more diet and health-conscious. They want the convenience of finger foods which gives them an alternative and allows them to make choices about what they're eating." . . .

Poultry food items account for about $300-million, or about half of the annual sales of all single-serving frozen food items sold nationwide in fast food restaurants and grocery stores, Baird says. Tyson estimates this year it will sell $1.5-billion dollars worth of nuggets and chunks to fast food chains or directly to consumers as frozen food products.

"The No. 1 entree at fast food restaurants is fried chicken," Baird says.

McDonald's representative Terri Capatosto declined to say what percentage of the company's total profits comes from McNugget sales. . . . McDonald's expected to sell 3.5-billion nuggets in 1984, the first full year the product was available nationwide. In fact, McNuggets have sold so well that, after their initial 12-week introduction, they propelled McDonald's into second place among chicken fast food restaurants.

"We concentrate on what we do best," Capatosto says. "McDonald's has run quality tests on the McNuggets, our customers have told us they enjoy the product and the nuggets have a lot of flavor.

"A hand-held chicken product, an 'on-the-go' item, appeals to everybody," she adds.

BUILDING A WRITING CONTEXT

1. **Why do people seem to be so fond of fast food chicken?**
2. **How do you think the reporter found information for her article?**
3. **Why are names and numbers important in an article like this?**

THE WRITING WORKSHOP

Preparing to Write

Often reporters gather information by taking a survey and then turning the results into an article. Brainstorm and write down questions that could be used to discover opinions and facts about chicken morsels in fast food restaurants.

What kinds of people could be questioned? What questions would:

- Encourage people to respond?
- Reveal their true feelings and opinions?
- Help build conclusions about the various products?

Once you have written your questions, class members can answer them to see how well they work. Make any needed changes. Then give your questionnaire to several different groups of people outside the class. For example, you could question: family members, members of another class in your school, people on a street in your community.

Developing the Writing

Now that you have a number of answers to your questions, you can begin composing your own article about chicken morsels in fast-food restaurants in your community.

- How will you structure your article?
- What point of view will you take?
- Will you write for an audience of students your own age, or a general audience from the community?
- How will you "load your evidence?" Will you be fair to each company or will you take sides?
- What anecdotes (little stories) will you include to make the reader want to continue reading?
- Will you use a graph or a table to help present the information?

Revising and Editing

A. Make up a title that represents your findings and will also create interest in the reader. Exchange your article with a classmate, and have him or her check to see if your writing flows along naturally from one point to the next. Make any needed changes.

B. If you have not already done so, write an interesting opening paragraph and then write a conclusion that ties the whole article together.

Sharing and Publishing

Your article should now be read by two or three people outside your class. Choose other students your own age, or people of different ages from the community. Ask them to comment on your information and style of writing. Record the readers' comments. By rereading your article and noticing the responses of those who read it, you can come to some conclusions about your effectiveness and skill in writing an article from a survey. Make any further changes that you feel will improve your article.

Growing from Writing

A. In a group, write a business letter to one of the companies that was mentioned in your survey.

Indicate in your letter the information you discovered, and give suggestions as to how this information might help the business — in sales, management, or public relations.

Mail or deliver your letter to the company's office or to the manager of the nearest outlet.

B. **Keeping a Journal**

Jot down your feelings and thoughts about fast food. You could use the following sentence beginnings:

I like______________________________________

I wish I didn't eat________________ because______________

____

I know I should eat______________________________

BUT I want to eat_______________________________

____

I will try to eat fast food only when____________________

____

____

Eyewitness Reports

The Young Samaritan

Each day you witness all kinds of events, yet you may hardly notice or remember them. Reporters, on the other hand, train their eyes to both observe and make sense of what they see. On this basis they prepare eyewitness reports. An eyewitness report usually combines an account of what is seen with the reactions of the one who has seen.

Yonge St. Samaritan Brightened My Day GARY LAUTENS

It's amazing how a stranger can touch your life. Let me give an example.

It was Yonge St. Early rush hour. And the sidewalk was crowded.

Kids, business people, . . . cops on beats, sidewalk hawkers, women rushing to get home, shoppers, the idle and the rich.

In short, a typical downtown scene.

Mad terrorists

I was walking home and (since we are being candid) feeling a little gloomy.

Incredible soccer riots. Awful faces of people attacking each other endlessly in the Middle East. Vandals in New York defacing subway cars before they're even in regular service. Mad terrorists on trial in Italy.

Sometimes you wonder if the whole world is crazy.

We talk of billions for Star Wars while thousands starve in Ethiopia. We don't worry about deficits while buying warplanes or new uniforms for soldiers, but we ask pensioners to take a pay cut. We pay $25 million to a man who throws a baseball, but can't find enough for cancer research.

Anyway, such dark thoughts were going through my head as I walked up the street.

Then it happened.

It was near the Dundas St. intersection.

A man with terrible physical handicaps was shuffling toward me, about a block away, when suddenly he fell.

Down he crashed to the pavement in a heap.

He just lay there, unable to help himself.

People in expensive suits, people with purple hair, people with earphones plugged into their heads, people with smart shopping bags, all kinds of people walked around him.

Maybe they didn't want to get involved. Maybe they were a little frightened by this man with his crippled body. Maybe they were caught up in their own thoughts and didn't notice.

Maybe it all happened too fast.

Fallen figure

Then out of nowhere a man appeared, a husky street guy who at a quick glance looked rather foreboding.

He bent over and gently picked up the fallen figure.

No fuss.

He steadied the man and asked if he was all right.

By then I was near enough to overhear the conversation. The handicapped man answered but it was very difficult to understand his reply.

The street guy nodded and went on.

It all took less than a minute.

Yonge St. went on about its noisy business. The handicapped man continued his painfully slow journey. And the Good Samaritan disappeared into the crowd.

The rest of the way home I thought about that simple act of kindness and somehow the outlook for humanity didn't look so bleak after all.

BUILDING A WRITING CONTEXT

1. **What did the writer actually see?**
2. **What were his feelings about what he saw?**
3. **What does the title refer to?**
4. **What effect do you think this eyewitness report has on most people who read it?**

THE WRITING WORKSHOP

Preparing to Write

As a class, watch an event taking place. It could be a sporting event, lunchtime in the cafeteria, or a big sale at a department store. Another possibility is to have a group of students from another class stage an event, such as a crime or an accident.

After watching the event, as a class discuss what happened. Record the details on the chalkboard. You may be surprised at the differences of opinion among class members as to what really happened. Training your eyes to see accurately is an important part of the writer's craft.

Developing the Writing

Write an eyewitness report. Choose an incident or situation to report on. Write your notes carefully. Record what you saw and heard, details of color and place, what things remind you of — anything having to do with the incident or situation.

Organize your information into an eyewitness report. This can take the form of a newspaper article. Another possibility is to try writing a court transcript. In this type of report, your evidence might be considered very important indeed.

Revising and Editing

In order to help you grasp how well you saw and heard details for your eyewitness reporting, have a partner read your report. Have your partner tell you in his or her own words what he or she thinks you said. If the two descriptions agree, then you have effectively described what you have seen. If not, revise your report in order to make it clearer and, if necessary, more complete.

Growing from Writing

Your eyewitness report can be the basis for poetry writing, since a poet — like a reporter — must use his or her eyes and ears to observe carefully.

Use information from your eyewitness report to write a poem that describes one action in great detail, as if you were putting it under a magnifying glass or seeing it in slow motion. Try to include the emotion you feel as you watch the action.

Example:

The Great Blue Heron
Fred Swayze

Deliberately
The great blue heron
Placed its food down deep into moss
And mud, anchoring each toe,
Delicately
Adjusted its weight and thrust of neck,
Its head like that of a striking snake,
And stepped again.
Imperceptibly
It approached the swaying lily pads
Where the little green frog blinked in the sun.
A white film
Slid across its eyes and was gone.
Then with intense concentration,
The clean bare bone of its bill poised,
It struck.

Formula Poems

Football Fingers

A formula poem is usually short, and written to a specific pattern or formula. Discovering the patterns used in these poems can be exciting. Writing poems using these formulas is an enjoyable way to begin poetry writing.

A. Acrostic

Magnificent
Always full of life
Reliable and kind
Yes, she's the greatest

This simple list poem is known as an *acrostic*. An acrostic poem looks something like a simple crossword puzzle. When you write an acrostic you use a person's name or the name of a place or object as your topic. Then for every letter in the word, you think of a word or group of words to tell about the topic.

Write an acrostic about yourself. Begin by writing your first name down the left side of your page. Think of adjectives that describe you, and that also begin with the correct letters as in the example above. You can write a second verse using your last name.

B. Four-Line Descriptive Model

Transport Truck
Patrick Lashmar

transport truck
tarnished and cranky
tackles the rugged mountain road
tenaciously

This form of list poem is known as a *four-line descriptive model.* The form is useful for writing descriptions that are brief yet forceful. Think about the characteristics of the pattern:

- The first line names the subject of the poem.
- The second line gives a visual description of the subject.
- The third line describes the action of the subject.
- The last line is one word, an adverb that catches the spirit of the subject.
- Also, each line begins with the same letter. This gives the poem an alliterative quality.

Write a four-line descriptive model, alone or with a partner. Use one of these subjects: hockey stick, rock star, wild horse, sports car.

C. Syllable Poem

Last Play of the Game
Patrick Lashmar

ball
cruising
cuts the mist
rain-coated fans
roar at the flanker
his wet fingers
beg the ball
pleading
score

The *syllable poem* is a nine-line form in which the number of syllables per line increases from one to five and back to one again. Alone or in a group of three, write a syllable poem on one of these topics: cat, homework, television, jet.

To begin, brainstorm a list of ideas and words that relate to your topic in some way. Then arrange them in a way that is both interesting and that follows the pattern outlined above.

D. Adverb Model

Sadly
Patrick Lashmar

Sadly the black line slowly
winds
Sadly the cold wind splits
the pines
Sadly the grave site dark
and cold
Sadly the truth — we all
grow old

This formula poem is called an *adverb model.* Notice that each line begins with the same adverb and that the poem is written in rhymed couplets.

With a partner write in this form using any topic you wish.

Sharing and Discussion

Do the following activities in a group of four.

1. Select one of the formula poems you have written and read it to your group. Tell the group what you like best about your poem. Other group members can tell what they like about the poems they read aloud.
2. Discuss the question "What is poetry?" Appoint a recorder to jot down your ideas and a presenter to present them.

THE WRITING WORKSHOP

Preparing to Write

Reread the formula poems and review the pattern for each. You will be writing several of these formula poems for members of your family to read. You will want your poems to interest your readers, perhaps by leading them to consider an ordinary idea in different ways.

Developing the Writing

1. Select a topic that interests you and develop it in four ways. Write an acrostic, a four-line descriptive model, an adverb model, and a syllable poem. Each poem should deal with a different aspect of your topic.
2. Once you select a topic, brainstorm words and ideas about it on a piece of paper. Next, you might organize these words and ideas around four subheadings. Each cluster of ideas could be used to compose one poem.
3. You might use an outline like the one below.

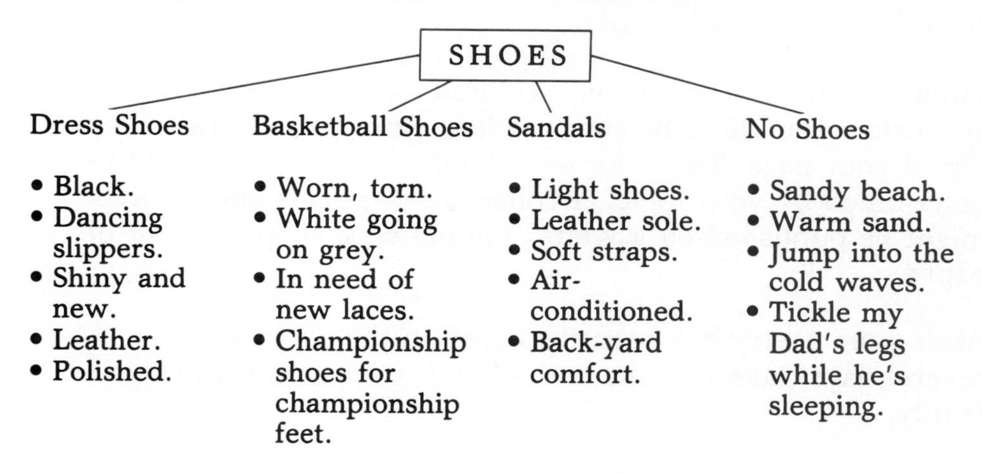

4. If your topic is *war*, you might develop a writing plan such as the following:
   - A Fierce Battle — an acrostic using the word *battle.*
   - A Tank — a four-line descriptive model to describe a tank.
   - Death of a Soldier — a syllable poem.
   - Peace — an adverb model using an adverb such as *finally, joyfully, peacefully.*

Revising and Editing

A. Read your four poems again and edit each as necessary using the questions below.

- Does my poem deal with my topic in an interesting, unusual, or powerful way?
- Are all my words and phrases specifically about the topic?
- Should I rearrange any of the ideas for a more powerful effect?

B. Precise Word Choice
One characteristic of good poetry is that it uses the fewest possible words to capture a situation.

Edit the poems written by another student. Focus on the words — what they say and how forcefully they say it. Suggest that all unnecessary words be left out. Remember, we are dealing here with poetry, not prose. Long grammatical structures are not necessary. Often one word can have a more powerful effect on a reader than an entire sentence.

Sharing and Publishing

Publish your four poems on a colored cut-out sheet. Add artwork if you wish. Be sure to place your overall title at the top of your page. The color and shape of the paper should be determined by your topic. A collection of poems about shoes might be published on a white running shoe shape cut out of paper.

After your poetry has been displayed in the classroom for several days, take it home and share it with members of your family.

Growing from Writing

By referring to several poetry anthologies, find five or six poems on the same topic you have written about. Encourage a classmate to read these along with the ones you have published. Later, have a discussion with your reader about how each poem relates effectively to the topic.

Free Verse

Good Morning, Sunshine

Small personal details — such as the time when you wake up, how you put on your slippers, who calls on the phone, what clothes you wear — actually make up a large part of your experience. They matter a lot, but they aren't usually put into poetry — they don't seem important enough. How can such things matter to anyone except the person who experiences them? Frank O'Hara puts them into his poetry for their own sake; they are simply there, as important as anything else.

Small details are obviously related to larger ideas and feelings, but the connection isn't insisted on. You get the feeling, reading Frank O'Hara, that anything and everything you think or see or feel can be put into a poem and it will work out right.

O'Hara's poems don't give deep explanations for the way life is — they give a feeling of what it's like to be alive. Have you had an experience with "the sun" as O'Hara had?

A True Account of
Talking to the Sun
at Fire Island
Frank O'Hara

The Sun woke me this morning loud
and clear, saying "Hey! I've been
trying to wake you up for fifteen
minutes. Don't be so rude, you are
only the second poet I've ever chosen
to speak to personally
so why
aren't you more attentive? If I could
burn you through the window I would
to wake you up. I can't hang around
here all day."
"Sorry, Sun, I stayed
up late last night talking to Hal."

"When I woke up Mayakovsky he was
a lot more prompt" the Sun said
petulantly. "Most people are up
already waiting to see if I'm going
to put in an appearance."

BUILDING A WRITING CONTEXT

1. **According to the poet, how did the sun feel when it finally woke him up? Why?**
2. **Why do you think nature seems so important to poets?**
3. **What kind of dream might the poet have had just before waking up?**

THE WRITING WORKSHOP

Preparing to Write

As a group, brainstorm instructions for having:
- A pleasant dream.
- A nightmare.

For example, what setting could be helpful to each kind of dream? What sounds could cause a person to experience these dreams?

Developing the Writing

Write a poem that has one of your own dreams in it. Start from anywhere — from a detail in the dream, or just from a thought. The important thing isn't to get the plot of the dream just right. The idea is to use the dream (some or all of it) to write a poem. Be as casual about the details of the dream as you are about your own thoughts.

As you write, let the poem be open to thoughts, associations, whatever comes to mind — even if it seems at the time trivial, strange, silly, incomplete, or disconnected. Whenever anything in the dream makes you think of something — an idea, a feeling a memory — write it down. Like O'Hara's poems, yours can be a combination of dreams and of thinking. One thing that might help you to get into a mood of dreamy concentration is to write while listening to music (Frank O'Hara often did this). Remember, nothing that you write has to be final — you can always change the poem later. Once you have polished it, you will have a chance to include it in a class book.

Revising and Editing

A. In a small group, read your poem aloud. Use a conversational tone as you read, as if the audience were eavesdropping.

B. Reading aloud may give you ideas about how you can improve your poem. Consider these suggestions:

- Can you arrange the lines differently, so that there will be more effective pauses?
- Can you use some asides (written inside brackets) to comment on what has happened, as if an inner voice is speaking to you?
- Can you divide your poems into several stanzas? Will you have any lines that repeat?

C. When poets use words whose sounds fit their meanings, we say they are using *onomatopoeia.* List several "sound" words that could be used in a poem; for example, *crunch, pitter-patter, whoosh, boom.*

Now reread your poem. Could you use onomatopoeia to make it even more effective? Try it.

Sharing and Publishing

Put together a class poetry collection called *Dreaming with Nature*. If some class members have photographic experience, black and white prints could be used to illustrate the poems.

Growing from Writing

A. Look through some science texts for an interesting description. Then arrange the lines into a "found poem" — a composition that, in a different context, has a feeling of poetic language.

B. Examine several travel ads. What is there about the writing that adds a poetic quality to the descriptions? What elements of poetry do ad writers use? Can you find any examples of onomatopoeia?

C. **Keeping a Journal**
If the sun spoke to you in the following situations, what would it say?

- You have a sunburn from your first day on the beach.
- You are hiding in the shade to keep cool.
- You are alone on an immense beach, far from home.
- An eclipse of the sun has just occurred.
- The sunset fills the sky with brilliance.

In your journal, write about "conversations" you might have with the sun in one or more of the above situations.

Narrative Poems

Arctic Trails Have Their Secret Tales

The poems you will be reading in this chapter are called narrative poems because each tells a story. A popular form of narrative poetry is the ballad. The ballad, one of the oldest forms of poetry, is still popular today. The ballads we enjoy today are usually recorded folk, country, or rock ballads.

Two of the poems in this chapter are ballads, meant to be sung. "The Battle of Queenston Heights" is an old Canadian ballad, while "Someday Soon" is a modern ballad. "The Cremation of Sam McGee" is a story poem, meant to be read aloud.

The Battle of Queenston Heights

Upon the Heights of Queenston one dark October day,
Invading foes were marshalled in battle's dread array.
Brave Brock looked up the rugged steep and planned a bold attack;
"No foreign flag shall float," said he, "above the Union Jack."

His loyal-hearted soldiers were ready every one,
Their foes were thrice their number, but duty must be done.
They started up the fire-swept hill with loud resounding cheers,
While Brock's inspiring voice rang out: "Push on, York Volunteers!"

But soon a fatal bullet pierced through his manly breast,
And loving friends to help him around the hero pressed;
''Push on,'' he said. ''Do not mind me!'' — and ere the set
of sun
Canadians held the rugged steep, the victory was won.

Each true Canadian soldier laments the death of Brock;
His country told its sorrow in monumental rock;
And if a foe should e'er invade our land in future years,
His dying words will guide us still: ''Push on, brave
Volunteers!''

Someday Soon
Ian Tyson

There's a young man that I know
His age is twenty-one
Comes from down in southern Colorado
He just got out of the service
And he's lookin' for his fun
Someday soon goin' with him
Someday soon.

My parents cannot stand him
Cause he rides the rodeo
My father says that he will leave me crying
I would follow him right down
The toughest road I know
Someday soon goin' with him
Someday soon.

And when he comes to call
My pa ain't got a good word to say
Guess it's cause he was just as wild
In his younger days
So blow you old blue northern
Blow my love to me
He's driving in tonight
From California
He loves his darn old rodeo
As much as he loves me
Someday soon goin' with him
Someday soon.

The Cremation of Sam McGee
Robert Service

There are strange things done in the midnight sun
By the men who moil for gold;
The Arctic trails have their secret tales
That would make your blood run cold;
The Northern Lights have seen queer sights,
But the queerest they ever did see
Was that night on the marge of Lake Lebarge
I cremated Sam McGee.

Now Sam McGee was from Tennessee, where the cotton blooms and blows.
Why he left his home in the South to roam 'round the Pole, God only knows.
He was always cold, but the land of gold seemed to hold him like a spell;
Though he'd often say in his homely way that 'he'd sooner live in hell.'

On a Christmas Day we were mushing our way over the Dawson trail.
Talk of your cold! Through the parka's fold it stabbed like a driven nail.
If our eyes we'd close, then the lashes froze till sometimes we couldn't see;
It wasn't much fun, but the only one to whimper was Sam McGee.

And that very night, as we lay packed tight in our robes beneath the snow,
And the dogs were fed, and the stars o'erhead were dancing heel and toe,
He turned to me, and 'Cap,' says he, 'I'll cash in this trip, I guess;
And if I do, I'm asking that you won't refuse my last request.'

Well, he seemed so low that I couldn't say no; then he says with a sort of moan;
'It's the cursed cold, and it's got right hold till I'm chilled clean through to the bone.

Yet 'tain't being dead — it's my awful dread of the icy grave that pains;
So I want you to swear that, foul or fair, you'll cremate my last remains.'

A pal's last need is a thing to heed, so I swore I would not fail;
And we started on at the streak of dawn; but God! he looked ghastly pale.
He crouched on the sleigh, and he raved all day of his home in Tennessee;
And before nightfall a corpse was all that was left of Sam McGee.

There wasn't a breath in that land of death, and I hurried, horror-driven,
With a corpse half hid that I couldn't get rid, because of a promise given;
It was lashed to the sleigh, and it seemed to say: 'You may tax your brawn and brains,
But you promised true, and it's up to you to cremate those last remains.'

Now a promise made is a debt unpaid, and the trail has its own stern code.
In the days to come, though my lips were dumb, in my heart how I cursed that load.
In the long, long night, by the lone firelight, while the huskies, round in a ring,
Howled out their woes to the homeless snows — O God! how I loathed the thing.

And every day that quiet clay seemed to heavy and heavier grow;
And on I went, though the dogs were spent and the grub was getting low;
The trail was bad, and I felt half mad, but I swore I would not give in;
And I'd often sing to the hateful thing, and it hearkened with a grin.

Till I came to the marge of Lake Lebarge, and a derelict there lay.

It was jammed in the ice, but I saw in a trice it was called
the 'Alice May.'
And I looked at it, and I thought a bit, and I looked at my
frozen chum;
Then 'Here,' said I, with a sudden cry, 'is my cre-ma-tor-eum.'

Some planks I tore from the cabin floor, and I lit the
boiler fire.
Some coal I found that was lying around, and I heaped
the fuel higher;
The flames just soared, and the furnace roared — such a
blaze you seldom see;
And I burrowed a hole in the glowing coal, and I stuffed
in Sam McGee.

Then I made a hike, for I didn't like to hear him sizzle so;
And the heavens scowled, and the huskies howled, and the
wind began to blow.
It was icy cold, but the hot sweat rolled down my cheeks,
and I don't know why;
And the greasy smoke in an inky cloak went streaking
down the sky.

I do not know how long in the snow I wrestled with grisly
fear;
But the stars came out and they danced about ere again I
ventured near;
I was sick with dread, but I bravely said: 'I'll just take a
peep inside.
I guess he's cooked, and it's time I looked'; . . . then the
door I opened wide.

And there sat Sam, looking cool and calm, in the heart of
the furnace roar;
And he wore a smile you could see a mile, and he said:
'Please close that door.
It's fine in here, but I greatly fear you'll let in the cold and
storm —
Since I left Plumtree, down in Tennessee, it's the first time
I've been warm.'

There are strange things done in the midnight sun
By the men who moil for gold;

The Arctic trails have their secret tales
That would make your blood run cold;
The Northern Lights have seen queer sights,
But the queerest they ever did see
Was that night on the marge of Lake Lebarge
I cremated Sam McGee.

BUILDING A WRITING CONTEXT

1. **List words and phrases from the ballad "The Battle of Queenston Heights" that describe General Brock in heroic terms. What do you know about the War of 1812, during which his heroic action took place?**
2. **Do you think the father's opinion of the boyfriend in "Someday Soon" is a fair one? Discuss this question with a partner or with the class.**
3. **Poets sometimes use exaggeration to create humor. From "The Cremation of Sam McGee," list examples of the use of exaggeration for humorous effects. Discuss your ideas with a partner or with the class.**

THE WRITING WORKSHOP

Preparing to Write

A. Ballads often have set patterns of rhyme and rhythm. Rhyme occurs when two or more lines of poetry end with the same final sound; for example:

On Christmas Day we were mushing our way over the
Dawson Trail.
Talk of your cold! Through the parka's fold it stabbed like
a driven nail.

In much of "The Cremation of Sam McGee," two lines in a row rhyme.

What is the pattern of rhyming lines in "The Battle of Queenston Heights?" Look back at the first stanza. Which lines rhyme in this stanza? Is the same pattern of rhyming used in the other four stanzas? Both "The Battle of Queenston Heights" and much of "The Cremation of Sam McGee" use what is known as an a a b b rhyme pattern. You will discover that many ballads use this pattern.

B. Rhythm is something like beat in music. Lines of poetry often have a set number of strong and weak syllables that produce the "beat;" for example:

The Arctic tráils have their secret táles
  That would make your blóod run cóld;

Each of these lines has two strong beats.

Developing the Writing

Now get ready to write your own ballad, using a regular rhyme and rhythm pattern. You will write it to entertain or to amuse your classmates. Your poem may be considered for publication in a class anthology.

1. Select a topic for your poem. Use one that is completely original, or work from one of the poems in this chapter. For example, you could:
   - Write a different ending for one of the poems in this chapter.
   - Write the same story from a different point of view.
2. Brainstorm the main ideas of your story. Then reread your ideas, adding, leaving out, or rearranging ideas as required.
3. In point form describe your main characters and your setting.
4. Now, using the points above, begin your first draft. If you get stuck because of your rhyme or rhythm pattern, just keep on writing anyway. You can work on rhyme and rhythm later.

Revising and Editing

A. Revise your poem using these questions:
- Should I add anything or leave anything out of my story to improve it?
- In my attempt to use a consistent rhyme and rhythm pattern, have I written some awkward-sounding lines, or lines that do not quite make sense? How can I improve these?

B. In groups of four, edit your poems focusing on the effective use of rhyme and rhythm.

Use these questions:
- Does the poem stay with the rhyme and rhythm pattern?
- Is the rhyme or rhythm "forced" in some places?
- Do the events in the story develop in an effective way?

C. Use the proofreading checklist on page 146 to proofread your poem before rewriting it.

Sharing and Publishing

Rewrite your narrative poem in your best handwriting. Keep it in your writing folder. Later you might want to submit it to a class anthology.

Growing from Writing

A. The speaker in the song "Someday Soon" says that her father was probably just as wild in his younger days as her boyfriend is now. Does this make the father's opinion of the boyfriend more or less valid? In one paragraph explain your point of view. Share your paragraph with a partner.

B. Bring recordings of modern ballads to class. These can be folk, country, or rock ballads that you enjoy. Listen to these in a group and talk about the story each tells.

C. Some ballads are especially suited to choral readings. In a small group, prepare a choral reading of part of "The Cremation of Sam McGee." Present your interpretation to the class.

D. With a partner make up a melody for "The Battle of Queenston Heights." Record your song on tape and play it for another group of students. If possible, have someone accompany you on a piano, guitar, or other instrument.

Lyric Poetry

Sing a Song of Seasons

A poet's deepest personal feelings are central to lyric poetry. The genius of the lyric poet lies in his or her ability to capture vivid experiences and strong emotions in words that sing.

In fact lyric poems were originally written to be sung. Modern song lyrics that are not chiefly narrative are sometimes excellent examples of lyric poetry.

Indian Summer
Wilfred Campbell

Along the line of smoky hills
The crimson forest stands,
And all the day the blue-jay calls
Throughout the autumn lands.

Now by the brook the maple leans
With all his glory spread,
And all the sumachs on the hills
Have turned their green to red.

Now by great marshes wrapt in mist,
Or past some river's mouth,
Throughout the long, still autumn day
Wild birds are flying south.

Pussywillows, Cat-tails
Gordon Lightfoot

Pussywillows, cat-tails, soft winds and roses,
Rain pools in the woodland water to my knees,
Shivering, quivering, the warm breath of spring.
Pussywillows, cat-tails, soft winds and roses.

Catbirds and cornfields, day dreams together,
Riding on the roadside, the dust gets in your eyes,
Leveling, disheveling, the summer winds can bring.
Pussywillows, cat-tails, soft winds and roses.

Slanted rays and coloured days, stark blue horizons,
Naked limbs and wheat-bins, hazy afternoons,
Voicing, rejoicing, the wine cups do bring
Pussywillows, cat-tails, soft winds and roses.

Harsh nights and candle lights, wood fires a-blazing,
Soft lips and fingertips resting in my soul.
Treasuring, remembering the promise of spring
Pussywillows, cat-tails, soft winds and roses.

BUILDING A WRITING CONTEXT

1. **The lyric "Indian Summer" appeals to our sense of sight. Which of its words and phrases are especially effective in creating pictures in your mind?**
2. **"Pussywillows, Cat-tails" captures the song-writer's experiences of the changing seasons. What season is being described in each verse?**
3. **What line in the fourth verse of "Pussywillows, Cat-tails" suggests that the cycle will continue?**
4. **What do you notice about the first two words of line three in each verse of "Pussywillows, Cat-tails?" Why do you think Lightfoot has done this? What does it add to the lyric?**
5. **If possible, listen to a recording of "Pussywillows, Cat-tails."**

THE WRITING WORKSHOP

Preparing to Write

When writing lyric poetry we should remember the following.

- The personal experiences and/or strong feelings being described are most important to lyric poetry. If the poem tells a story as well, the story should be secondary.
- Imagination is important. Try using unusual or imaginative methods to describe your experiences or feelings.
- Although lyric poetry does not need to have definite rhythm or stanza patterns, the lines should still have a musical quality about them.

Developing the Writing

1. Brainstorm possible topics or experiences in one list and strong emotions in another. When you are satisfied with your lists, match particular feelings with specific topics or experiences. The partial lists below may help you get started.

Topic/Experience/Idea	*Strong Emotions*
lawnmower	joy
going to war	worry
October	peace
snake	fear
snow	love
watering the lawn	delight
________________	________________

2. Once you select a topic or experience with an appropriate strong emotion that you would like to work into a poem, brainstorm a list of words, phrases, and comparisons that somehow describe this emotion and/or the topic or experience. Example:
   watering the lawn ——————— joy
   - Hose is a bright green skipping rope.
   - Hose laughs and sprays the children.
   - Bright, hot July afternoon.
   - Happy, laughing children.
   - Spray like a gentle waterfall.

3. Now take your topic, the feeling you want to convey, and your brainstormed list of words and phrases. Work these into a lyric poem.

Revising and Editing

Edit your poem with a partner. Help one another to make your poems clear and interesting. Use the following questions.

- Is the strong feeling I'm trying to communicate clear?
- Is the topic described in an unusual way?
- Are the comparisons that I used colorful and interesting?
- Should I add more ideas, leave some out, or rearrange ideas to express my impressions and feelings more effectively?

Sharing and Publishing

In groups of six take turns reading your poems aloud. Practice your oral reading beforehand. For each poem the group can discuss the main emotion being described and talk about what parts of the description were most interesting. Write your final draft in your best handwriting and keep it in your writing folder.

Growing from Writing

A. "Indian Summer" has been studied in schools for many years. One reason for its popularity is the fact that it is an ideal poem to recite or read aloud. The clear images the poem presents and its regular form make this poem easy to memorize. Read the poem several times aloud until you feel you understand it well. Then memorize the poem and prepare to recite it. In groups of four, take turns reciting this poem. Perhaps you will want to recite it for the class or another group.

B. In "Pussywillows, Cat-tails," Lightfoot has written four highly descriptive verses to describe the seasons — spring, summer, autumn, winter. Decide which season you like best, and write a descriptive paragraph about it. Remember that your task is not to narrate; that is, to tell a story, but rather to paint a clear, accurate picture. Use your knowledge of careful word choice. Write and rewrite your paragraph until you are satisfied that you have described your favorite season as well as you are able. Then you could share your paragraph with a group of classmates.

Essays

Helen Keller's Dream

A well-written essay has a plan. To write a good essay, you have to think your way through your subject, decide the approach you are going to take, and work out a rough outline, either in writing or just in your mind.

The following essay by Helen Keller is easy to read and understand because there is a plan to the writing.

Helen Keller was born in Alabama in 1880. When she was 19 months old she became blind and deaf. Through her teacher, Anne Sullivan, she learned to speak and read by touch and feel. She began formal schooling at 14, went to college, and graduated from university at 24. Helen Keller wrote her first book, *The Story of My Life*, while at college. She also wrote many other books and articles. Because of her energy and enthusiasm, she became an inspiration and force in furthering the cause of the world's deaf and blind people. Helen Keller died in 1968.

Three Days to See HELEN KELLER

I have often thought it would be a blessing if each human being were stricken blind and deaf for a few days at some time during . . . early adult life. Darkness would make him or her more appreciative of sight; silence would teach . . . the joys of sound.

Now and then I have tested my seeing friends to discover what they see. Recently I asked a friend, who had just returned from a long walk in the woods, what she had observed. "Nothing in particular," she replied. I was astonished.

How was it possible, I asked myself, to walk for an hour through the woods and see nothing worthy of note? I who cannot see find hundreds of things to interest me through mere touch. I feel the delicate symmetry of a leaf. I pass my hands lovingly about the smooth skin of a silver birch, or the rough, shaggy bark of a pine. In spring I touch the branches of trees hopefully in search of a bud, the first sign of awakening nature after her winter's sleep. Occasionally, if I am very fortunate, I place my hand gently on a small tree and feel the happy quiver of a bird in full song.

At times my heart cries out with longing to see all these things. If I can get so much pleasure from mere touch, how much more beauty must be revealed by sight. And I have imagined, selecting carefully, what I should most like to see if I were given the use of my eyes, say, for just a three-day period.

I should divide the period into three parts. On the first day, I should want to see the people whose kindness and companionship have made my life worth living. I do not know what it is to see into the heart of a friend through that "window of the soul," the eye. I can only "see" through my finger tips the outline of a face. . . .

The first day would be a busy one. I should call to me all my dear friends and look long into their faces, imprinting upon my mind the outward evidences of the beauty that is within them. I should let my eyes rest, too, on the face of a baby, so that I could catch a vision of the eager, innocent beauty which precedes the individual's consciousness of the conflicts which life develops. I should like to see the books which have been read to me, and which have revealed to me the deepest channels of human life. And I should like to look into the loyal, trusting eyes of my dogs, the little Scottie and the stalwart Great Dane.

In the afternoon I should take a long walk in the woods and intoxicate my eyes on the beauties of the world of nature. And I should pray for the glory of a colourful sunset. That night, I think, I should not be able to sleep.

The next day I should arise with the dawn and see the thrilling miracle by which night is transformed into day. I should behold with awe the magnificent panorama of light with which the sun awakens the sleeping earth.

This day I should devote to a hasty glimpse of the world, past and present. I should want to see the pageant of human progress and so I should go to the museums. There my eyes would see the condensed history of the earth — animals and the races of people pictured in their native environment; gigantic carcasses of dinosaurs and mastodons which roamed the earth before people appeared. . . .

My next stop would be the museum of art. I know well through my hands the sculptured gods and goddesses of the ancient Nile land. I have felt copies of Parthenon friezes and I have sensed the rhythmic beauty of charging Athenian warriors. The gnarled, bearded features of Homer are dear to me, for he, too, knew blindness. . . .

The evening of my second day I should spend at a theater or at the movies. How I should like to see the fascinating figure of Hamlet, or the gusty Falstaff and colorful Elizabethan trappings! . . .

The following morning I should again greet the dawn, anxious to discover new delights, new revelations of beauty. Today, this third day, I shall spend in the workaday world, amid the haunts of people going about the business of life. The city becomes my destination. There I must go at once!

First, I stand at a busy corner merely looking at people, trying by sight of them to understand something of their daily lives. I see smiles and I am happy. I see serious determination and I am proud. I see suffering and I am compassionate.

From Fifth Avenue I make a tour of the city — to the slums, to factories, to parks where children play. I take a stay-at-home trip abroad by visiting the foreign quarters. Always my eyes are open wide to all the sights of both happiness and misery so that I may probe deep and add to my understanding of how people work and live.

My third day of sight is drawing to an end. Perhaps there are many serious pursuits to which I should devote the few remaining hours, but I am afraid that on the evening of that last day I should again run away to the theater, to a hilariously funny play, so that I might appreciate the overtones of comedy in the human spirit.

At midnight permanent night would close in on me again. Naturally in those three short days I should not have seen all I wanted to see. Only when darkness had again descended upon me should I realize how much I had left unseen.

Perhaps this short outline does not agree with the program you might set for yourself if you knew that you were about to be stricken blind. I am, however, sure that if you faced that fate, you would use your eyes as never before. Everything you saw would become dear to you. Your eyes would touch and embrace every object that came within your range of vision. Then, at last, you would really see, and a new world of beauty would open itself before you.

BUILDING A WRITING CONTEXT

1. **Do you feel that Helen Keller is correct in saying that those of us with the senses of sight and hearing do not really appreciate these senses? Write down three ways in which you could use them better.**
2. **Use five numbered headings to list the five main parts of this essay. You could begin as follows.**
   I. Introduction
   II. First Day
3. **Under each of your five headings, list two to four main points of the essay. You could begin as follows.**
   I. Introduction
      A. Being blind and deaf for a few days would make people appreciate sight and sound.
      B. Some people don't seem to appreciate their senses.
      C. I dream of being sighted for just three days.

THE WRITING WORKSHOP

Preparing to Write

Learning to write an essay outline is useful, but dangerous. Often a writer becomes so involved in the form of an outline that he or she stops thinking of the writing being outlined.

Yet a reader needs some form, or he or she may become confused, get lost, or give up. As you begin, you may find a direction — even a conclusion — flowering in your mind. Then all you need to do is find examples, experiences, and details to bring it alive and flesh it out.

To construct a good piece of writing, you need to be going somewhere in it. If you aren't taking a journey in your own mind, no amount of outlining or structuring can make your writing live. Your writing must contain surprises and questions, or else it will remain dead for both you and the reader.

How much planning will you do before you start writing an essay? This will depend largely on the kind of person you are. You may feel most comfortable developing a detailed outline first. On the other hand, you may do your best writing if you simply keep a general outline in mind.

No matter which kind of writer you are, it is well to be aware of the three main parts of an essay:

- Introduction — one or more paragraphs including statement of essay's main idea.
- Development — several paragraphs explaining and expanding on the main idea.
- Conclusion — one or more paragraphs summing up the essay, and usually restating the main idea in a somewhat different way.

Developing the Writing

A. Ezra Pound, a well-known writer and literary critic, once said, "It doesn't matter which leg of your table you make first, so long as the table has four legs and will stand up solidly when you have finished it."

Write a paragraph relating this statement to the idea of the importance of organizing one's writing.

B. In the introduction to her essay, Helen Keller briefly told of an incident: her friend walked in the woods but later said she had seen nothing in particular. Choose three of the following topics. Write brief incidents that you could use in introductions to essays about these topics.

- Three days of hearing for a deaf person.
- A fictional character I'd like to meet.
- The children of my relatives.
- Blue Monday mood.
- A popular movie I didn't like.
- Names: advantages and disadvantages.

- Effects of weather on my thoughts.
- Things I could get along without.
- The secret of a successful camping trip.

C. Every essay needs a main idea, or theme. For example, the main idea of an essay on the secret of a successful camping trip could be: Plan ahead but keep your sense of humor even if things don't go as planned. Write main ideas, or themes, you could use for three of the essay topics listed in Activity B above.

D. Choose a topic from Activity B, or decide on an essay topic of your own. Then go ahead and write your essay. If you feel a written outline would help you, prepare one before you start writing. If not, simply make plans in your mind and use them as a guide while you write. Feel free to change your plans as you write.

Revising and Editing

Reread your essay. Look for any places where it is not clear when one event comes before another, or causes something else to happen. Make adjustments to clarify your sequence and cause/effect relationships. Useful signal words to use would include:

- first
- next
- then
- finally
- since
- caused by
- as a result
- if — then
- consequently
- because
- for this reason
- therefore

Growing from Writing

Look over a piece of writing done earlier this school year. (You may find a suitable one in your writing folder.) Can you improve this piece of writing with a firmer pattern of development? Go ahead and do it.

Parodies

Did You See My Shopping List?

Every year, "Ten Best" lists appear in journals and newspapers. People choose their favorite items, from restaurants to rock stars. The lists can be arranged consecutively, chronologically, or randomly, but the end product must have impact.

The following selection is a parody of list writers. It pokes fun at this type of writing by imitating it.

The People V. Jim GARRISON KEILLOR

Q: Jim, I'd like you to look at this magazine article entitled "The Twenty Best Hash Browns in Town" and tell me if you wrote it.

A: Yes, I did.

Q: How about this? "Fifteen Great Ideas for Putting New Life in Those Dingy Stair Treads." Was that the second "list" article you wrote for a magazine?

A: No, that was my tenth. That was after "Eleven Restaurants You'll Remember the Rest of Your Life," "Ten All-Time Greatest Half & Halfs," "My Ten All-Time Favorite People," "Ten Ways to Lose Four Pounds in Two Days," "Ten Celebrities Show Off Their Basements," "Eight Methods of Beating the Heat," "Seven Terrific Marriages," "Six Meaner Dogs Than You Ever Saw Before," and "Five Kids Who Make Your Kids Look Sick."

Q: What happened, Jim? Why couldn't you quit then? You knew it was wrong.

A: I know, but look at it my way. First of all, I think that —

Q: "Thirty People Who'd Like to Be Your Friend," "Ten Famous Peoples' Breakfasts," "Eighteen Best Red Things," "Six Best Tops of Things," "Twelve Biggest Unnoticed Things," "Twenty-one Places Where Famous People Were Seen Doing One of Two Things" — the list goes on, Jim. . .

A: Lists helped to center me a little, calm me down. I took out a clean sheet of paper, numbered it from one to fifteen or twenty — I got a feeling of accomplishment.

Q: You went crazy, Jim. You wrote for sixty-eight different life-style magazines, . . . and you wrote lists of best artists, best music videos, best hamburgers, quiet restaurants, noisy restaurants, bourbons, aluminum foils, dining-room sets, wallets, American novels, cheese snacks, hotel lobbies, movies, women named Diane, burritos, "Ten Most Exciting Elevators," "Ten Cures for Winter Arghhs," "Ten People Who Have Something You'll Never Have," "Ten Things That Look Very Unusual But Really Aren't," "Ten Things You Don't Need to Worry About," "Ten Places Nearby That You Ought to Drop Everything and Go Look at Immediately," "The Thirty-nine Most Successful, Restless, Desperately Unhappy People in West Virginia," "Fifty Top U.S. Businesses Run by Methodists" — surely, Jim, there must have come a point when you thought, That is enough. I can't do this anymore.

A: I had filled up sixty-one floppy discs by then. I wanted to reach a hundred.

Q: So you filled your hundredth disc, and you collected everything in "The Fatal List," and it reached No. 8 on the *Times* list, and then —?

A: I was ready to retire, but the editor of *Milwaukeeist* told me to cough up ten more, otherwise he would include me in "Fifty People Who Were Once Hot and Aren't Anymore for One Reason or Another." So I did them.

Q: Do you have any idea what damage you've done, Jim? You've made people more stupid. Some of your readers now find it hard to read paragraphs that aren't numbered.

A: How many? A lot?

Q: Jim, we're going to have to put you in a little room by yourself for a while, I think.

A: Will I ever write again?
Q: No.

BUILDING A WRITING CONTEXT

1. **Which of the imaginary articles could actually have been written?**
2. **Which ones would you like to read?**
3. **How does the author use exaggeration to help create humor?**

THE WRITING WORKSHOP

Preparing to Write

Who can take life seriously all the time? Have you ever imitated a family member, joked about a TV commercial, or drawn a cartoon of a neighbor? Such parodies are "jokes on life." They often make us feel a lot better about people and situations that we can't do much about.

The world of television often likes to make fun of itself by creating humorous sketches that are spoofs or parodies of different programs. *The Carol Burnett Show* and *SCTV* are particularly noted for this type of humor.

Developing the Writing

For this assignment you will be working as a group to create a parody of a type of TV program. By exaggerating and imitating the characters and situations, you will be mocking some of the absurdities and obvious things we often see on TV.

As a group, choose a program you would like to parody. It could be a game show, a soap opera, a cooking show, an interview show, a favorite situation comedy, a show for young children, or any other.

Once your group has made a choice, work together to write out a script for a five-minute parody that could be used as a sketch on a comedy show. Here are some questions to consider as you write.

1. Do you want to poke fun at the characters, the situations, or both?

2. What specific words should you include to give your work "reality"?
3. What ideas are basic to the type of show you have chosen? These will serve as a model for your own writing.

Change the title of your program from the original, but retain enough meaning so that the reader will understand what you are parodying.

Revising and Editing

A simple way of observing the effect of your parody is to have it read aloud and to assess the reader's response. This type of feedback will help you know which areas in your writing need to be altered, clarified, exaggerated, or described in greater detail.

You may want to complete your final draft in the form of a script, using a style similar to that of "The People V. Jim" at the beginning of this chapter.

Sharing and Publishing

Your parodies should be shared and enjoyed. Groups may want to dramatize some of the class's parodies for others to watch. Your class could organize a "parody review," bringing to life the works you have created.

Growing from Writing

A. Think of a popular television commercial that you could parody. Working with a partner, create a script for a one-minute commercial. You could make fun of the product, characters, or style of selling. You could also write a parody of the song, slogan, or jingle that accompanies this commercial.

Once you have prepared the script, work with your partner to act it out. Consider having a "crazy commercial" day in your class.

B. Create a parody of some type of newspaper writing. Here are some suggestions for your humorous "take-off."
- A letter to an advice columnist.
- A weather report.
- A description of a sports event.

- A description of a fashion show.
- Ripley's Believe It or Not.
- Horoscopes.

C. Create a parody of a test you might receive in school. It could be a math, history, science, or general trivia test. Perhaps you could write true-false questions, fill-in-the-blanks questions, short-answer questions, and/or multiple choice questions in which the answers are quite obvious. Examples:

- The day after yesterday is ________________.
- How long did the Seven Years War last?

Expository Paragraphs

Four on the Floor

An expository paragraph is often composed of a group of sentences expressing one central idea. A paragraph may be complete in itself, and yet also a subdivision or part of something larger, such as an essay or report.

Unless it is at the beginning of a piece of writing, a paragraph begins with a space called an *indentation.* A piece of writing composed of several paragraphs will have several indentations — making it easy for the reader to see where each new paragraph begins.

Expository writing often explains or proves a point. What point is being made in each of the following expository paragraphs?

from Zephyr JEAN LITTLE

The writer is a well-known Canadian author with limited vision. Zephyr is her Seeing Eye dog.

I am certain that Zephyr likes his life to have a purpose. I am further convinced that he regards dogs who are mere pets with some sympathy and much condescension. "Spoiled and useless, poor things!" I have almost heard him comment as he passes them by, and shows off his special harness. He trots along so cockily, his tail curled up and swinging buoyantly in time with his gait, his nose in the air. I myself have told him that he belongs in the proud company of working dogs: dogs who herd animals, dogs who go hunting, dogs who guard buildings, dogs who rescue people lost in the snow, dogs who let deaf people know when their baby cries or their doorbell rings. If he has concluded that dogs who guide and protect blind people are the most important working dogs of all, that is not my fault. I must admit though that I find this bias wholly forgivable.

from the introduction to Forty Acres *by Mark Day* CESAR CHAVEZ

The writer has dedicated much of his life to creating better conditions for farmworkers.

I have often been asked what kind of a union I am trying to build and what type of society I want to see in the future. It seems to me that, once the union members are taken care of in terms of better wages and working conditions, the union must involve itself in the major issues of the times. The problem often arises that a group gets too involved in its own successes and doesn't have time for anything else. It is my hope that we keep ourselves focused on our ideals. It is much easier to profess something by words and not by deeds. Our job, then, is to educate our members so that they will be conscious of the needs of others less fortunate than themselves. The scope of the worker's interest must motivate him to reach out and help others. If we can get across the idea of participating in other causes, then we have real education.

BUILDING A WRITING CONTEXT

1. **In each of these paragraphs, the author states the main idea in the first sentence. List two details that help support Jean Little's main idea. Then list two details that help support the main idea of Cesar Chavez' paragraph.**

2. **Why do both these authors use the pronoun *I* in their paragraphs? In what kinds of writing might it not be appropriate to write in the first person (using the pronoun *I*)?**
3. **How does Jean Little help us understand what the word *condescension* means?**

THE WRITING WORKSHOP

Preparing to Write

A. An effective paragraph contains only relevant facts and ideas, arranged in the clearest possible order. Expository paragraphs generally have the following basic elements:

1. *One central idea.* A paragraph is a group of closely related sentences that develop and clarify one, and only one, central idea. Carefully select the material you include in a paragraph so that you don't stray from its central idea. Sentences that point in several different directions rather than towards a single idea will only confuse your reader.
2. *Topic sentence.* The topic sentence is the most important sentence in a paragraph. A topic sentence indicates what the paragraph is about. It is often but not necessarily the first sentence in the paragraph. The topic sentence helps the writer decide what to include and exclude. Only information that develops or clarifies the idea stated in the topic sentence belongs in the paragraph.
3. *Specific details.* Most successful expository paragraphs contain several specific details that develop and clarify the idea expressed in the topic sentence. These details may include such things as facts, figures, thoughts, observations, steps, listings, quotations, examples, and personal experiences.

B. Although a well-developed paragraph contains a generous supply of specific details, it is not enough to present them in whatever order they happen to come to mind. There are several common patterns for paragraph development:

1. *General to specific.* The writer begins with a general statement — the topic sentence — and then moves to specific statements that explain or support it.

2. *Specific to general.* The writer begins with specific statements and then concludes with a general statement, the topic sentence.
3. *Time sequence.* If writing about events, the writer often arranges them in chronological order — that is, in the order in which they happen.
4. *Space sequence.* If writing about objects, the writer often presents them in an orderly arrangement that enables the reader to see how the objects relate to one another physically — that is, in space; for example, from top to bottom, from left to right, from near by to far away.

Developing the Writing

A. Working in a group of 3-5 students, write a paragraph following the steps below.

1. Choose a subject that all members of the group know something about. Example:
   - The school's best team.
   - The joys (sorrows) of being a teenager.
   - A car we would never own.
   - Why we'd change a certain rule in our school.
   - One of our favorite television shows.
2. Compose a topic sentence about this subject, making sure it is narrow enough to be covered in detail in one paragraph.
3. Jointly make a list of developing details that support, explain, illustrate, or illuminate the topic sentence.
4. Agree on the best order for these details.
5. Check to make sure all details are relevant to the topic sentence.
6. Compose the sentences containing the developmental details.
7. Have one member of the group check the paragraph for spelling, punctuation, usage, and final form.
8. Exchange paragraphs with another group and evaluate each other's work.

B. Write a paragraph that develops one of the following ideas. Use the *general to specific* method of development described in the Preparing to Write section. Underline your topic sentence.

- One quality necessary for success is______________________.
- To me, the most attractive career would be ______________.
- The best (or worst) thing about fast food restaurants is _____.

- The quality I most admire in a person is ________________.
- What I most enjoy doing in my spare time is ________________.
- Sometimes a student can't help feeling that he or she is regarded as a number, not a person.
- Nothing can beat a country walk on a nice day.

C. Write a paragraph beginning with one of the following groups of words. Use the *specific to general* approach described in the Preparing to Write section.
- I hated it when . . .
- I loved it when . . .
- I don't think it's fair that . . .
- Why should I have to . . .
- It made me laugh when . . .
- I cried when . . .
- My parents got mad when . . .

D. Have you ever visited a park that seemed truly a model of the kind of park a city should provide for its citizens? In a well-written paragraph, describe it in detail, concentrating on a few outstanding features. Use the *space sequence* approach described in the Preparing to Write section.

Revising and Editing

A. The sentences within a paragraph should be linked to one another in ways that make them flow smoothly and enable the reader to easily follow the progression of thought. This may be accomplished through the use of linking devices such as the following.

1. *Connecting words and phrases.* Here are some of the most commonly used connecting words and phrases, grouped according to the relationships they show.
   - Similarity: likewise, similarly.
   - Contrast: on the other hand, on the contrary, at the same time, otherwise, however, nevertheless, but, yet, still.
   - Result or effect: since, consequently, accordingly, hence, thus, as a result, therefore, because, if.
   - Adding ideas together: first, in the first place, second, and also, furthermore, too, moreover, also, in addition, finally, in conclusion.

- Providing emphasis or clarity: that is, in other words, again, as a matter of fact, in fact, indeed, nonetheless, besides, although, after all, above all.
- Indicating time relationship: later, until, while, meanwhile, now, from now on, next, after, afterwards, at times, once, when, then, subsequently.
- Introducing an example: for example, for instance, to illustrate.
- Conceding a point: of course, granted that, to be sure.

2. *Repetition of words and phrases.* Repetition of key words and phrases in several sentences of a paragraph is another way to help the reader follow the train of thought.
3. *Use of pronouns and demonstrative adjectives.* Pronouns point back to nouns or pronouns that appear earlier in the sentence, or in previous sentences. Thus they pull sentences closer together and help guide the reader along a continuous path. Example:
   - Dr. Mahler is considerate of *his* patients. *He* cares about *their* comfort.

   There are four demonstrative adjectives: *this, that, these,* and *those*. All are special adjectives that identify nouns. Example:
   - *This* plane belongs to *that* pilot.

B. Examine the paragraphs you wrote in this chapter to see if they would profit from the insertion of more linking devices. Put a checkmark at any point in a paragraph where such a device would help. Write the linking word or phrase in the margin to the left of the line. Include the linking words and phrases in the final drafts of your paragraphs.

Growing from Writing

Select a movie you have just seen or a book you have just read. Write a paragraph to persuade one of your friends to see the movie or read the book. Then write another paragraph on the the same book or movie, but this time try to persuade one of your parents. Then analyze the two paragraphs to see how having a different audience influenced your paragraph development.

Time Capsules

What Time Is the Next Stage?

It can be fun to look at history by examining a "time capsule" — a brief record of a period of time encapsulated in a few words. Only the highlights are touched upon, but you do get the flavor of the times. The following time capsule takes a look at "the western" movie as it developed over 100 years.

Stages of the Western

1870
Buffalo Bill Cody presents his Wild West Show to the east; stars Wild Bill Hickock. . .

1908-14
Broncho Billy (G.M. Anderson) stars in 375 Westerns; budget for each film is about $800; there is little continuity, if Billy dies one week, he returns the next.

1909
The Western is established — IN OLD ARIZONA, AN INDIAN'S SOLITUDE, BOOTS AND SADDLES, IN THE BADLANDS, CUSTER'S LAST STAND, ON THE BORDER, THE TENDERFOOT. . .

1917
Tom Mix — a simple character, carefree, never smokes, drinks, or cusses (on screen); wears a big white hat; 1917 SIX-CYLINDER LOVE, 1922 JUST TONY, NO MAN'S GOLD, 1935 THE MIRACLE RIDER (this is shown as a serial on TV in the 50's). . .

1923

John Cruze THE COVERED WAGON — first epic Western, costs $750,000; 10 reels long, shot on location; little historical authenticity, but it amazes the audience by its size and splendor; it breaks attendance records.

TWO WAGONS – BOTH COVERED — parody by Will Rogers. . .

1930's

The Big Westerns — 1930 THE BIG TRAIL, BILLY THE KID, 1931 CIMARRON, 1932 LAW AND ORDER.

The "B" Westerns emerge — simple films of action.

At the end of the decade, Hollywood is making 500 feature films a year, 100 of them Westerns.

The Western serial is established — Gene Autry, The Lone Ranger, Hopalong Cassidy, Zorro.

The singing cowboys — Roy Rogers, Gene Autry, Dick Foran, Tex Ritter, Jimmy Wakely, Eddie Dean. . .

1930

THE UTAH KID — stars Boris Karloff. . .

1939

COLORADO SUNSET — "The musical Western at its most lunatic — showgirls, politics and the west incongruously interwoven."

STAGECOACH — John Wayne's career is launched.

THE OKLAHOMA KID — James Cagney and Humphrey Bogart laugh at each other in their cowboy outfits.

The cult of the outlaw — JESSIE JAMES, WHEN THE DALTONS RIDE, BILLY THE KID, BADMEN OF THE MISSOURI (the Younger brothers), THE RETURN OF FRANK JAMES, WESTERN UNION.

1940

THE WESTERNER — Walter Brennan wins his third Academy Award.

1943

THE OX-BOW INCIDENT — the first social-protest Western. . .

1950's

Psychological Westerns — 1950 WINCHESTER '73, 1953 SHANE, 1956 THE SEARCHERS. . .

1952

HIGH NOON – Gary Cooper wins an Academy Award.

1958

THE LEFT-HANDED GUN — Paul Newman.

1960's
Sympathy for the Indian — 1964 CHEYENNE AUTUMN, 1969 TELL THEM WILLIE BOY IS HERE, 1970 A MAN CALLED HORSE, 1971 LITTLE BIG MAN; but still no Western from the Indian's point of view.
Satires on the Western — 1965 CAT BALLOU, 1969 TRUE GRIT, BUTCH CASSIDY AND THE SUNDANCE KID. . .

1963
HOW THE WEST WAS WON — Cinerama; the biggest box-office Western.

1967
The spaghetti Westerns — movies made in Spain, by Italians, and dubbed into English.

1969
THE WILD BUNCH — the most violent Western to date; about outlaws who had outlived the old west.

BUILDING A WRITING CONTEXT

1. **Which of the films mentioned have you seen?**
2. **How do you think real cowboys differ from those shown in movies over the years?**
3. **Do you think "the western" has been replaced by any other type of film today? What type?**

THE WRITING WORKSHOP

Preparing to Write

A time capsule is a convenient way to arrange information in time order. You can design time capsules to look like charts or calendars. People enjoy reading time capsules because they give a great deal of information very quickly. In other words, a time capsule gives an overview.

Developing the Writing

Create a time capsule of your years in school — from kindergarten to your present grade.

1. Begin by writing down your strongest memories of school — teachers, classmates, lessons, free time, bus rides, excursions,

supply teachers, Teachers' Convention days, parties, exams, homework, and so on. Do this at random, because one memory will trigger another.

2. When you are finished, go back over your list, adding any new images and thoughts that occur to you. You can write them between the lines or in the margins. The idea is to write down as many ideas and memories as possible.
3. Read your lists (unorganized) to each other in small groups so that you can hitchhike on each other's memories. What happened to others can be the basis for triggering your own memories. When you have added these new thoughts to your brainstormed list, you can begin to organize your time capsule.
4. Decide who your readers will be. If you are writing for your parents and/or other adults, they will be looking for and interested in certain details. If you are writing for fellow students, they may be interested in different sorts of information.
5. Write your time capsule for your intended readers.

Sharing and Publishing

When you have written your time capsule, give it to your intended audience to read. Observe how effective your style is.

If you wish, ask your readers for comments and suggestions for improvement. Revise your time capsule, taking their suggestions into consideration.

Growing from Writing

A. Create a time capsule as an "end of year" project for your teacher and/or family.

B. Make a time capsule as a "good-bye card" for someone who is moving away.

C. Use a time capsule to record your own progress in a particular field, such as sports or cooking, in which your skills develop by stages.

Maps and Atlases

Face of the Earth

People have drawn maps since at least 5000 B.C. About that time, maps showing the extent of Mesopotamia were scratched into the surface of clay tablets. These tablets show mountains, water bodies, and other geographic features. It is thought that portions of the Nile valley were carefully mapped in ancient times in order to recover property lines after the annual floods. Also, travellers used maps to plot courses or routes.

One modern activity that calls for the use of maps is a kind of cross-country racing called *orienteering*. This is a sport that is fairly new. The following selection tells how a few students put their map-reading skills to use by going through an orienteering course.

Follow Me — I'm an Orienteer

MARY MARTENS

Stuart and his Grandma were trying to drive to Sandhills Park but they kept losing their way. "Look at the map!" Grandma kept telling Stuart. "I have to keep my eyes on the road. Which way do I turn? How far are we from the park? Are we north or south of highway 77? Are we supposed to cross the Rouge River?"

Poor Stuart had to admit he was puzzled. He stared and stared at the map, but he couldn't seem to answer all of Grandma's questions. Finally they met a park ranger, who led them to Sandhills Park in his truck.

Next day Stuart discussed the experience with some of his

classmates. ''I know how you must have felt,'' said Tracy. ''When our family goes on holidays, we always get into arguments about how to read the map and where we're supposed to go.''

The teacher, Ms. Koryzna, had been listening to the conversation. ''Maybe this would be a good time for our class to go orienteering,'' she suggested.

There was silence for a moment. ''Does that have anything to do with China or Japan?'' asked Rosa. ''We already studied them last year.''

''You're thinking of the Orient,'' said Ms. Koryzna. ''No, the word *orienteering* comes from the same Latin root, but it means *finding your way* or *finding your directions*.''

''Guess that's what I need,'' mumbled Stuart, sliding into his seat.

''There's a course laid out for orienteering near Robsart's Mill,'' said Ms. Koryzna. ''Let's meet there tomorrow morning and try it.''

At the mill Ms. Koryzna divided the class into groups of five. She gave each group a compass and a map of the orienteering course. Each group had seven control points marked on its map, with a short explanation beside each. The control points were different for each group.

''This orienteering course has many control points,'' explained Ms. Koryzna. ''But I've chosen only seven for each group, since we're beginners.''

''That's for sure,'' said Tracy, puzzling over her group's map.

''Each time you reach one of the control points,'' said Ms. Koryzna, ''you'll find a small blue sign with a code word on it. You write the code word beside the control point on your map.''

''Aha!'' said Dirk. ''The secret code word proves we really found the control point.''

''I guess it's something like a treasure hunt,'' observed Wynne.

''Right,'' said their teacher. ''OK, are you ready? The first group to come back with its seven correct code words is the winner.''

Stuart and his group read the clue beside their closest control point: ''Downhill to wooden gate, northwest through forest to grey boulder.''

''Oh no!'' groaned Cindy as they began jogging through the forest. ''Look at all the boulders. How will we know when we get to the right one?''

The whole group was stumped for a moment. Then Wynne thought of looking at the map scale. "See, on this map a centimeter stands for .25 km."

"It's about half a centimeter from the gate to the boulder," observed Nathan. "That means we have to go about an eighth of a kilometer. Come on, let's hurry."

Sure enough, after about .12 km, Stuart's group found the first control point. Wynne quickly wrote the code word on their map: *isthmus.*

"Hey, we're good at this!" exclaimed Cindy.

"I wouldn't say that just yet," said Stuart. "Look at this next explanation: 'Use compass bearing 125° to lone tree stump by shallow stream.'"

"Um ... I think we've got to start by facing north," said Jan. "See, the moss is thicker on *that* side of the tree trunks. That must be north."

"Yeah, that's the way the compass needle points," said Nathan. "But how do we —?"

"I know!" interrupted Stuart. "We turn the numbers so the needle's at zero. Then we go the way the needle *would* point if it were at 125°."

Nathan grinned. "Hey, you're a better orienteer than I thought, Stu."

Using the compass the group found their second control point and second code word: *dendrite.*

After crossing the stream, Stuart and the others were puzzled about how to reach their third control point, a beaver dam. Should they follow the path or the road? Both seemed to lead in the right direction, but one could easily turn off before it reached the dam.

At last Cindy thought of looking at the map legend. "According to this," she said, "a double line means a road, and a single line means a path."

Stuart peered at the map. "So that means we follow the path, not the road. "Hurry up, gang."

Less than an hour later, Stuart and his group were back at the mill. "You did very well," said Ms. Koryzna after checking their map and seven code words. "You're the third group back, and all your code words are right."

Stuart grinned. "Hey, just wait till my Grandma hears about this!"

BUILDING A WRITING CONTEXT

1. **Does orienteering sound like a "fun" event? Give reasons for your answer.**
2. **Could a group of students like yourself put together an orienteering course? What would you need to do a good job?**

THE WRITING WORKSHOP

Preparing to Write

A map is a drawing representing the earth's surface or a part of it. Even the most "realistic" map, however, does not show the earth exactly the way a bird sees it. Many maps present invisible or abstract information that even the most perceptive bird could never see. For example, they show the equator and lines of latitude and longitude, which are actually not visible on the earth's surface.

Today, maps take many forms. They are often printed in multiple colors by high-speed presses, or are stored in the memory banks of computers. The topics they depict range from the topography of the ocean floor to the pattern of crime rates in a particular city.

Developing the Writing

A. Look at a map of the United States and locate ten different geographical elements. Examples: river, lake, town, city, border, boundary, state, capital city. Note the symbols used for some of these.

B. Using two maps of different scale, compute the distance from your community to Chicago, Illinois. Compare the results in paragraph form.

C. Plan a trip using a road map to show distance, directions, and the locations of points of interest. Describe your planned journey in paragraph form. Include a copy of the map, showing your intended route.

D. Draw a picture of your room, pretending you are looking down through a hole in the ceiling. Be sure to draw all four walls, to show where the door is, and to show the tops of all the things in your room. This drawing will be a sort of map.

E. Hundreds of years ago, many a pirate buried gold and jewels on a lonely island. Of course, the pirate would draw a map so that he could find the treasure again when he went back to the island. Yet some pirates never made it back to their treasure islands.

Pretend you have found a pirate map in an old trunk. Draw it. If the reader can follow your directions exactly, he or she can find the way to the buried treasure. You should indicate directions, sketches, and interesting names for the varied geography: cove, beach, lake, plateau, forest, cave, mountain, brook, treasure.

F. Take a large piece of paper and a pencil and walk around your neighborhood, sketching in streets and buildings. Share your map with your classmates. Discuss how you simplified drawings and, in some cases, turned them into symbols.

Growing from Writing

You can use maps in written reports and oral presentations to help you illustrate the information you are discussing. It is often easier for people to understand something when they see it, rather than just read or hear about it. A visual aid such as a map can provide several kinds of information at a glance, helping the listener make connections among the facts you are presenting.

Plan a short report in which you will use a map to help illustrate your points. Narrow down the topic you have chosen to a workable statement of purpose. Your statement of purpose will help focus your entire report. It will help you select the material and maps you need to include. Leave out material that does not relate to your specific topic. Suggestions for a subject would include:

- A famous historical event. Example: the battle of Gettysburg.
- Current events. Examples: a kidnapping, an oil spill.
- Biography of a famous person. The lives of famous people can be made more vivid to your readers or listeners by the use of maps.

- Literature. When you are doing a book report, a map could help explain special features of the work being discussed. It could help illustrate the book's events.
- Personal experience. Examples: traffic accidents, getting lost, visiting another country, going on a field trip, visiting a park.

After you have given your presentation, ask your listeners if they have any questions about any point you have not made clear.

RESEARCH

Giving Information

The Dog Ate My Homework

Often when junior high school students think of school, they think of school discipline. Indeed, many adults think that discipline is the number one problem facing schools today.

The following selection (not meant to be taken seriously) is a "tongue-in-cheek" description of how some students behave in school. What are some results of such behavior? In what ways does it interfere with learning?

How to Behave at School DELIA EPHRON

Ma, I don't feel good. Maybe I shouldn't get up today. I feel sorta blah. I don't know — I just feel yucky all over. Ma? Ma, would you feel my forehead? I don't? Are you sure? Are you positive? OK, I'll get up. I'll get up, but you'll see — I'll probably just get to school and have to turn around and come home again.

Arrive at school late. Explain that you are tardy because you couldn't find your shoe.

As soon as the teacher turns to write on the blackboard, open your desk, pull out a magazine, and put it inside the language arts workbook. Read magazine while it looks as if you are reading language arts. . . .

Whisper. Stop when the teacher asks if you'd prefer to spend class in the hall. Ask to change your seat.

Pretend that your pencils are ships; steer them around your desk and make them collide. Look at the clock.

When the teacher asks for a volunteer to take names while she is out of the classroom, raise your hand, shake it frantically, stretch so that your body is nearly a horizontal line between your desk and the teacher, and call out, "Me, me, me, me, me, me, me." You do not get chosen.

What to Do While the Teacher Is Out of the Classroom: Hold your nose and say in a high-pitched voice, "Now class, behave." Run to the front of the room and draw your fingernails down the blackboard. Return to your seat like Groucho Marx, hunched over, looking both ways, wiggling eyebrows, and chomping on a pencil as if it were a cigar. Get your name taken.

Get it erased by threatening to get the name-taker at recess.

Sail a paper airplane and when it lands, raise your hands, clasp them above one shoulder, then the other. You are the champ. Get your name taken.

Throw an eraser. . . .

Ask to get something from your coat in the cloakroom.

Ask to sharpen your pencil.

Tell the teacher, for the second time this week, that you do not have your homework because the dog ate it. She will say that if this kind of behavior continues, she will have to note it on your permanent record card.

Look at the clock.

Ask to get a drink of water.

In the Hall

Look in all the classrooms you pass, stopping at one or two long enough to attract attention and distract the students — stick thumbs in ears and wave fingers, or scratch armpits like a monkey and heave up and down. If a class has its door closed, jump up to see through the window on the door. Play hopscotch, using floor tiles as squares. Stand against the wall and inch your way down the hall — you are in a spy movie. When you reach a corner, peek around it. After turning up the water at the fountain to see how high it will go, fill up your squirt gun. Walk back to class with the point of the gun in your mouth, keep pulling the trigger.

As soon as you return, check the clock to see how much time you killed.

BUILDING A WRITING CONTEXT

1. **Why is the introduction to this article written in italics?**
2. **What does the method of presentation (giving directions) add to the humor of the article?**
3. **Explain how the following might cause school discipline problems: students' personal problems, fear of failure, lack of motivation, family problems.**
4. **How do you think the following might help solve school discipline problems: greater contact between parents and schools, help from advisors and counselors, more teacher training, more respect for others on the part of students, better understanding of the values and goals of education?**

THE WRITING WORKSHOP

Preparing to Write

There are two main attributes of good writing, to which all other qualities are related. Good writing is interesting to read, and it is written with technical skill.

The first and most basic requirement we make of anything we read is that it interest and/or entertain us. Good writers create and keep the interest of their readers. Secondly, they show their technical skill in such matters as using accurate effective words; including specific details that appeal to the senses; and observing the accepted conventions of spelling, punctuation, grammar, and usage.

Developing the Writing

A. Two rules to observe for more effective writing are:
- Reject all unnecessary words.
- Add words only as they contribute to meaning.

Rewrite the following paragraph, considering the rules above.

In our times in the modern world of today, mechanical machines have taken over the occupations and jobs of some people of the human race and deprived those human beings of their former employment. Yet in addition we human beings must not forget to remember that through the ages or periods of history machines or gadgets that take the place of human hands have continually been discovered or invented.

B. In a small group, brainstorm some of the following questions. Then select one and ask for more indepth opinions from your group members. Finally, develop the topic in several paragraphs.

1. What age would you like to be for the rest of your life?
2. If you lost everything you own, what would you do?
3. What would be the most effective ways of improving discipline in schools?
4. If you could choose one place to live the rest of your life, where would it be?
5. If you had just 24 hours to live, how would you spend them?
6. What would be the advantages and disadvantages of living life as a hermit?

Revising and Editing

Reread your paragraphs, thinking about the following questions. Make any necessary improvements.

1. Have I chosen a topic I know well?
2. Have I narrowed the subject adequately?
3. Does my main idea statement indicate that I have taken a point of view in relation to the subject?
4. Is my main idea statement precise?
5. Is my writing logically organized?
6. Does my writing contain extra material that does not support or amplify the main idea?
7. Does my piece of writing have an effective conclusion?

Sharing and Publishing

Share your writing by reading it aloud to the group with whom you discussed the topics before beginning to write. In your group talk about your writing and how your ideas have developed since you first started discussing the topics.

Growing from Writing

A. Does your school have an official set of rules? If so, read and discuss them in a group. If not, work as a group to write some rules you feel would serve as a basis for the most effective learning situation possible in your school.

B. Find out something about the school system of another country such as England, Germany, China, India, or France. Perhaps you could do research by speaking with people from those countries and/or consulting encyclopedias and other books. Write a brief report on how schools in the other country differ from your school. Include some opinions on what we might learn from the schools of the other country, and what they might learn from ours.

Exam Responses

True or False

Not exams again! A possibly frustrating activity you face as a student is writing examinations and tests. Here are some general day-to-day suggestions that may help.

- **Do each day's school work carefully, and correct the mistakes you make.**
- **Keep a notebook in which to write important notes for review.**
- **If you do not understand something in a lesson, get help immediately. Be sure that rules, formulas, and new words have meaning for you.**
- **Memorize important facts.**
- **Sometimes study with a friend or family member, so you can discuss problems together.**
- **The night before a test, go to bed early and get a good night's sleep.**

"The subject was inexplicable, so I didn't try to explick it."

"Here's my test, Mr. Sauer. I've left a few intentional mistakes. I wonder if you'll be able to find them."

BUILDING A WRITING CONTEXT

1. What point is each cartoon making?
2. Which cartoons do you find funniest? Why?

THE WRITING WORKSHOP

Preparing to Write

You know an exam is coming soon. What specific things can you do?

A. Memorize Essential Terms

To help you remember specific names, you might make up an acrostic — a special word or sentence in which the first letter of each word is the same as the first letter of each term you want to memorize. Examples:

- "HOMES" could help you remember the names of the five great lakes: Huron, Ontario, Michigan, Erie, Superior.
- "Many very early mermaids just sat under navy parasols" could remind you of the order of the planets from the sun: Mercury, Venus, Earth, Mars, Jupiter, Saturn, Uranus, Neptune, Pluto.
- "Every good boy deserves figs" could remind you of the notes represented by the lines of a musical staff: EGBDF.

B. **Review**

The first time you review your notes or reread your textbook, underline the important points. Mark important dates, and names and titles of significant people. Underline major technical terms. (If you are not allowed to write in your book, take notes on paper.) After you've marked your book and notes, you need review only the underlined material. Review at least once a week.

C. **Determine the Nature of the Exam**

Sometimes the teacher will drop hints or even make outright statements about what's coming up on a test. You may be able to find out if the exam will be mainly objective or essay, what areas you should concentrate on, and how much the quality of writing will count.

D. **Test Yourself**

- Write down a list of all the important terms, names, and so on. (You can also use the table of contents of your textbook or the subheads in a chapter as your list of cues.) Then, without looking at the book or your notes, think of all the important points you can about each name or term.
- Next take your list and ask yourself: What kinds of questions would I ask on these topics if I were the teacher? Then answer those questions.
- Make flash cards for yourself, with a question or vocabulary term on one side and the answer on the other. This kind of pretesting can be more enjoyable if you study with others from your class. When you choose study companions, be sure they are serious about the work. It's easy to let a study group turn into a goofing-off group.

E. **Writing the Exam**

- In a true-false question, if a statement is partly false, mark it false.
- Remember that *all, only, always,* and *never* mean *without any exceptions.*
- Watch for words like *usually, often* and *frequently*, which may change the character of the answer required.
- For a multiple-choice question, eliminate choices which you know are wrong, and then choose from those that are left.

- For a multiple-choice question, you could also try to think of the answer before you look at the choices available. Finish the question yourself in the way that seems most logical. Then, when you look at the choices, the right one may jump out at you.
- Do the easier questions first. As you look through the exam, you'll notice that some answers flash into your mind right away. On other questions, however, you'll find your brain drawing a blank. Don't get bogged down on questions for which your mind went blank. First do all the questions you find easiest. You may want to put a small mark next to those you skip. After you finish the easier ones, go back to the others.

Developing the Writing

A. Make up acrostics to help you remember each of the following.

- The names of U.S. time zones from west to east: Pacific, Mountain, Central, Eastern.
- The names of important glands in the body: pituitary, thyroid, adrenal, salivary, sweat, digestive.
- Most people know the acrostic ROY G. BIV, which helps us remember the colors of the rainbow: red, orange, yellow, green, blue, indigo, violet. Make up another acrostic for these colors.

B. Join a group of 4 or 5 classmates. Together choose a section of one of your textbooks, perhaps 6 or 7 pages long. Each group member then works alone to make notes on this section. Write down the most important points, as if you were preparing for an exam. When everyone has finished, share the results and talk about them. What can you learn from the other group members? Do your notes include all the important points? How can you tell if a point is important or not? Are your notes too long? Too short?

C. This time, work alone. Choose another section in one of your textbooks, perhaps 6 or 7 pages long. As you read it, write down 3 or 4 exam-type questions requiring written answers. Now close your textbook. Write answers to your own questions. When you have finished, check back with the textbook to see how well you did. You may wish to give yourself a grade such as 60% or 70%.

Revising and Editing

When writing an exam, always proofread your answers if time permits. Too many students race through their exams and leave before time is up. Remember, you have worked all year or all semester on that particular course. Use every minute available to help you achieve as high a mark as possible. Check and, if time permits, doublecheck your work.

Growing from Writing

A. In a group, choose a chapter or unit of study that the class has recently completed. It may be in language arts, science, social studies, or some other subject area. In your group, compose questions based on this chapter or unit. Try to include several different kinds of objective questions, such as multiple choice, true/false, and fill-in-the-blanks. Examples:

- *Multiple choice*
  Choose the best completion for each statement.
  1. The formula for converting a Fahrenheit temperature to Celsius is
     a. °F − 32 × 5/9 = °C
     b. °F × 5 + 9 = °C
     c. °F × 5/9 + 32 = °C

- *True/false*
  Write T if the statement is true. Write F if it is false.
  1. Both dates and coconuts come from palm trees.
  2. Cocoa is made from the bark of a kind of pine tree.

- *Fill-in-the-blanks*
  In each blank write the word or group of words that best completes the statement.
  1. The first U.S. President was ____________________.
  2. ________________ was the last state to join the Union.

Ask your teacher to administer the exam to the class. Afterwards your teacher can go through the results with you, discussing the strong and weak points of your various questions.

B. Knowing the types of questions you will be asked can help you prepare for an exam.

Following are a number of differences between questions in which the student writes only very short answers or selects answers from a number of choices (objective questions) and questions in which the student writes longer answers (subjective questions). Read the following statements and, in your notebook, jot down whether each statement applies to objective questions or subjective questions.

1. Require the student to plan the answer.
2. Questions are specific and numerous.
3. Questions are general and relatively few in number.
4. Students spend most of their time thinking and writing.
5. Students spend most of their time reading and thinking.
6. Afford much freedom for the student to express his or her individuality and depth of understanding.
7. Afford little freedom for the student to express his or her individuality and depth of understanding.
8. Permit and may actually encourage guessing.
9. Relatively quick and easy to mark.
10. Marking takes time and good judgment.

Business Letters

To the Office of the Mayor

Business letters use a special form and type of language basic to written communications in the world of business. The most important rule in writing a business letter is to get to the point immediately. Do not use vague language or a cluttered style. Business letters have special purposes — such as to sell a product or service, to collect money, to explain an idea, or to win a friend. Every word must do its job.

Writing business letters is a challenge! You must persuade on paper — getting across the facts with creativity, clarity, and courtesy.

The following example was written by a student.

Millgrove School
2609 Grove Avenue
Mayfield, Illinois
26017

Mayor George Cuff
Office of the Mayor
130 Spruce Street
Mayfield, Illinois
26017

Dear Mr. Cuff:
My classmates and I would like to thank you very much for the time you took in visiting our class. We also thank you for showing us the video and telling us more about Mayfield becoming a city. I am now convinced that the fact that we are becoming a city is not bad, but good.

Many students in my class now feel more comfortable about the situation of Mayfield becoming a city. So, thank you again for coming to speak to our class.

Yours very truly,

Lesley Cameron

Lesley Cameron

BUILDING A WRITING CONTEXT

1. **In what ways are business letters unlike friendly letters?**
2. **In a business letter, why should your style be as brief and clear as possible?**
3. **Where does the letter-writer's address go in a business letter? Why is the letter-receiver's address included? Where does it go? How are these addresses punctuated?**
4. **Pick out the other parts of the letter: salutation, body, complimentary closing, handwritten signature, typed signature. How are they positioned and punctuated?**

THE WRITING WORKSHOP

Preparing to Write

In day-to-day life, there are many occasions for which we might write business letters. For example, if you dislike an article in a newspaper or magazine because it doesn't "tell it like it is," or you feel so strongly about a certain issue that you want to influence others, you can write a letter to the editor.

This simple device is an illustration of what democracy is all about. However, just as there is no guarantee that your letter will, in fact, persuade people, there is also no guarantee that your letter will even be published. Your chances will be improved, however, if you follow some common-sense rules.

1. Be prepared. Pick out some letters that you find particularly interesting and then ask yourself why these letters captured your attention.
2. Be brief. Get to the point fast and in no uncertain terms — in the first sentence.
3. Be relevant. Once you've made your point, don't wander from subject to subject. Don't clutter your letter with extra material.
4. Use moderation. Be sensible and realistic. Don't overdo it by gushing, raging, whining, and so on.
5. Emphasize facts. Support your opinions with facts.
6. Call for action. After you've made your point and supported it with facts, call for some definite action by the group or person involved in the subject of your letter.
7. Write promptly. Letters to daily newspapers should be mailed within a day of the article or editorial that prompted them.

Developing the Writing

A. Write a letter to the editor of your local newspaper discussing one of the following aspects of school life in your community.

- What makes a course popular with students.
- The place of science in education.
- Some reasons students fail exams.
- I'd prefer to attend an old-fashioned one-room school.

- Sex education should be compulsory.
- Some advantages of a student's life.
- Extracurricular activities in my school.
- A deficiency in education.
- Can a smart student fail?
- Who deserves an education?
- Red tape in schools.
- Students are smarter than teachers believe.
- Vacations are too short (or too long).
- Schools try to do too much.
- A fad in our school.
- Things I'll never forget about my education.

B. A sales letter is a business letter that attempts to persuade the reader to action by an appeal to his or her self-interest, such as:

- To make money.
- To save time.
- To avoid effort.
- To gratify curiosity.
- To satisfy a need.
- To protect reputation.
- To protect family.
- To be popular.
- To be healthy.
- To be comfortable.

Look at some sales ads in the local newspaper. Then write a sales letter to a possible customer. Try to sell a particular product by appealing to one or more of the above self-interests.

C. Choose one of the following subjects and write a letter of apology.

1. You have lost a book borrowed from the local library. (Supply the title and author of the book and state what you intend to do about the loss.)
2. You have been taking a course in a foreign language from a special school in your community. You want to discontinue the lessons and are also inquiring about a possible refund of the balance of your tuition fee. (Name the language and give the reason(s) why you are stopping the lessons.)
3. You have changed your mind about a reservation in a motel in a resort area over the Christmas holiday. You would like to cancel the reservation and have your deposit refunded. (Supply the name of the motel, the dates of the reservation, and the amount of money you deposited.)

Revising and Editing

There are 6 basic "Cs" of effective business letters. Reread the letter or letters you have just written. Revise and edit according to the following points:

1. Clarity (clearness) is the quality of being understood. Clear writing results from clear thinking.
   - Arrange ideas in logical order.
   - Use as few words as you can to express your meaning.
   - Be sure pronouns refer clearly to the nouns intended.
   - Be sure there are no "double meanings."
2. Correctness. Take time to be sure. Check and recheck — physical makeup of letter (spacing, etc.), spelling, grammar — anything that might waste the reader's time or cause misunderstanding.
3. Creativeness. Use as interesting an approach as you can, while still remaining businesslike.
4. Completeness. Be sure the letter covers all the essential information needed for complete understanding of the message.
5. Compactness. Brevity shows that the writer fully understands what he or she is writing about. It also avoids wasting the reader's valuable time.
6. Consideration. Showing courtesy in expression goes a long way towards building a favourable image, for yourself and/or a company.

Sharing and Publishing

Consider actually mailing one or more of the letters you have written.

Growing from Writing

A. Many letters of application result in job interviews. Below are reasons that employers often give for rejecting job applicants. As you read the following reasons, ask yourself how you would rate in relation to each.

1. Late to interview without good reason.
2. Poor personal appearance.
3. Lack of confidence and poise, nervousness, ill at ease.
4. Never heard of company.
5. High-pressure type.

6. Overbearing, overaggressive, conceited, "know-it-all" attitude.
7. Indefinite response to questions.
8. Inability to express himself or herself clearly.
9. Lack of interest and enthusiasm — passive, indifferent.
10. Makes excuses, is evasive, hedges.
11. Lack of courtesy — ill-mannered.
12. Lack of social understanding.
13. Friction with parents.
14. Unhappy personal life.
15. Fails to look interviewer in the eye.
16. Little sense of humor.
17. Low moral standards.
18. Cynical.
19. Lazy.
20. Intolerant, strong prejudices.
21. Narrow interests.
22. Asks no questions about the job.
23. Poor scholastic record — just got by.
24. Unwilling to start at the bottom; expects too much too soon.
25. Overemphasis on money — interested only in best dollar offer.
26. Condemnation of past employers.
27. Sloppy application form.
28. Merely shopping around.
29. Wants job only for short time.
30. Emphasis on whom he or she knows.
31. No interest in community activities.
32. Radical ideas.
33. Inability to take criticism.
34. Failure to express appreciation for interviewer's time.

B. Write a memorandum to yourself — "for your eyes only." Tell yourself how you could improve with respect to the rejection reasons listed. This could be important to you in seeking a part-time or summer job. Taking a long-range view, it could also be important for a fulltime occupation sometime in the future.

C. Write a script in which an employer interviews two job applicants, one after the other. One applicant has mostly positive qualities. The other has several of the negative qualities indicated in the list.

REVISION CHECKLISTS

Content Checklist

1. Will my writing interest my readers?
2. Did I say everything I wanted to say?
3. Did I say it the way I wanted to say it?
4. Did I say it clearly so that others will understand what I wrote?
5. Did I stay on topic throughout my piece of writing?
6. Did I include all the necessary information?
7. Should I leave some ideas out?
8. Should I change some of my ideas?
9. Did I write the events, ideas, and/or steps in a logical order?
10. If I was asked to follow a pattern, did I do it well?
11. Did I use comparisons when appropriate to make my work more interesting and more accurate?
12. Did I write a good beginning, middle, and end?
13. If writing a paragraph, did I write a strong topic sentence? Do all the sentences in the paragraph belong with the topic sentence? Did I write an effective closing sentence? Did I organize the sentences in the best order?
14. Did I vary my sentence types and constructions?
15. Did I use the most accurate and interesting words that I could think of?

Proofreading Checklist

1. Does each sentence make sense?
2. Does the order of words in each sentence make sense?
3. If a sentence is too long, how can I change it to make two or more shorter sentences? If some sentences are too short, how can I combine them?
4. Is my grammar correct?
5. Have I punctuated each sentence correctly?
6. Have I used capital letters correctly?
7. Where I have used direct speech, have I punctuated it correctly?
8. Did I spell words correctly, checking those about which I was unsure?
9. Did I use proper form with regard to indenting, titles, and margins?
10. Is my writing clear and easy to read?

Author/Title Index

Subject Index

Acknowledgments

Every effort has been made to acknowledge all sources of material used in this book. The publishers would be grateful if any errors or omissions were pointed out, so that they may be corrected.

Acknowledgment is gratefully made for the use of the following copyright material: "To Be Rich...Or Poor" from *Children's Express*. Reprinted by permission of Dorriet Kavanaugh, Workman Publishing Co. and Children's Express. "The Wedding Party" from *The Comedy World of Stan Laurel* by John McCabe. Reprinted by permission of Doubleday & Company, Inc. From *Nobody's Family is Going to Change* by Louise Fitzhugh, copyright © 1974 by Louise Fitzhugh. Reprinted by permission of Delacorte Press, a division of Bantam, Doubleday, Dell Publishing Group, Inc. Excerpt from "Land of the Gopher" by Eric Nicol. Reprinted by permission of McGraw-Hill Ryerson Limited. Excerpt from *August 2026: There Will Come Soft Rains* by Ray Bradbury. Reprinted by permission of Don Congdon Associates, Inc. Copyright © 1950 by Ray Bradbury, Renewed 1977 by Ray Bradbury. "There Will Come Soft Rains" by Sara Teasdale. Reprinted with permission of Macmillan Publishing Company from *Collected Poems* by Sara Teasdale. Copyright 1920 by Macmillan Publishing Company, renewed 1948 by Mamie T. Whalesa. "The Railroad Ghost" by Murray T. Pringle. Copyright 1954 Story Parade, Inc. Copyright renewed 1983. Reprinted by permission of Western Publishing Company, Inc. "Sleep" from *Klee Wyck* by Emily Carr © 1941 Clarke, Irwin & Co. Ltd. Used by permission of Irwin Publishing Inc. Excerpt from *The Diary of Anne Frank* by Anne Frank. Reprinted by permission of Vallentine Mitchell & Co. Ltd. "Mean Song" from *It Doesn't Always Have to Rhyme* by Eve Merriam. Copyright © 1962 by Eve Merriam. All rights reserved. Reprinted by permission of Marian Reiner for the author. "New dragon will surface this month" reprinted by permission of *The Chronicle-Herald* and *The Mail-Star*. "With a Little Bit of Pluck" by Mary Haley in St. Petersburg Times. Reprinted by permission of Mary Haley. "Yonge St. Samaritan brightened my day" by Gary Lautens. Reprinted with permission — The Toronto Star Syndicate. "The Cremation of Sam McGee" by Robert W. Service. © Dodd Mead & Co. 1907, Used by Permission Estate of Robert Service. Excerpt from *Three Days to See* by Helen Keller. Copyright 1933 by Helen Keller. Reprinted by permission of Doubleday & Company, Inc. Introduction by Cesar Chavez from *Forty Acres: Cesar Chavez and The Farm Workers* by Mark Day, copyright © 1971 by Mark Day, reprinted by permission of Henry Holt and Company, Inc. Excerpt from *Zephyr* by Jean Little to be published in 1987. "Follow Me — I'm an Orienteer" by Mary Martens. Reprinted by permission of the author. "How to Behave at School" from *How to Eat Like a Child* by Delia Ephron, 1977, 1978. Reprinted by permission of Viking Penguin, Inc.